Replic

and

Open Communication

As Methods of Finding the Truth

PHILLIP K. TOMPKINS

outskirts press

Outskirts Press, Inc.
http://www.outskirtspress.com

ISBN: 978-1-9772-4296-9

PRINTED IN THE UNITED STATES OF AMERICA

Dedicated

to

Emily

For all that

is so

lovingly

done

Table of Contents

Preface

Before explaining my reasons for writing this book, let me introduce myself: I am a Professor Emeritus, Communication and Comparative Literature, University of Colorado at Boulder. Most folks call me Phil. In 1962 my Ph.D. degree was earned while studying a new field called Organizational Communication created at Purdue University. The chief founder of the new field, Professor W. Charles Redding, was my doctoral academic adviser.

After a satisfying career I retired in 1998. Since retiring I have worked as a volunteer at the St. Francis Center, a large day shelter for homeless people in Denver. In that same time span, I also wrote four books that have been published, two of which are about homelessness. Another is about the United States Space Program and the fourth is about the management of risk and complexity.

I was extraordinarily fortunate in my early thirties to have had two experiences that taught me two powerful methods of learning the truth: replication and open communication. I used one or the other at work in subsequent research projects described in separate chapters of this book.

The first of the two cases, the replication of an experiment in a chemistry lab, was discussed in my first faculty meeting. Sound dull? The Dean of the Graduate School who called and chaired the meeting in which it was introduced said it was the saddest moment of his career.

The second occasion was the honor bestowed on me when I was made the first "soft scientist" to serve as a Summer Faculty Consultant to Dr. Wernher von Braun, Director of NASA's Marshall Space Flight Center. He was regarded as the most brilliant rocket scientist of the time. In 1967, he was managing the Research and Development of the Saturn V, the Rocket intended to take us to the Moon, and back.

Dr. von Braun learned by experience and keen observation that organizational communication was as important as the science and engineering knowledge he applied to his projects. He asked me to conduct a diagnostic study of his organization, MSFC, to find out "what works and what does not." I spent that summer of 1967 doing so by means of in-depth interviews up and down the hierarchy. I came away with absolute amazement at the brilliant, original communication practices Dr. von Braun and his colleagues had developed. They would later become my model of "Open Communication." In 1968, I was called back by the Marshall Space Flight Center to replicate parts of my 1967 diagnostic study and to help find out which space ventures to pursue after Apollo. In subsequent years I did two more studies at NASA, on Challenger and Columbia.

In the rest of my career, I used replication and open communication in my research projects, classroom teaching, and in my daily life. The ones mentioned in this Preface are included in chapters of this book: In 1966, I practiced replication for the first time, not in a chemistry lab, but by researching and writing an article published in *Esquire* magazine proving that a best-selling book by a famous author *did not tell the truth*. I had a bit more than fifteen minutes of fame as a result.

In 1970, I was asked to replicate the methodology of the NASA diagnostic study at Kent State University to discover why it had been necessary to call in the National Guard and why the song, "Four Dead in Ohio" was written. The publisher of the book about our KSU study went out of business shortly after issuing barely a handful of copies of our book, co-authored by the young woman who has been my wife ever since. For that reason, few people know that we learned organizational communication problems caused that tragedy. In 1971 I was asked to replicate the Kent State diagnostic study at the State University of New York at Albany as the new Chair of their Department of Rhetoric and Communication.

For this book I also did some library research on "second opinions" in medicine, research in the field of Psychology, and part of a chapter focusing on a Canadian artist by the name of Rick Ducommun. Rick had read my most recent book: *Managing Risk and Communication through Open Communication and Teamwork,* published by the Purdue University Press in 2015. He presented me with two small paintings inspired by that book. He gave me permission to use them in this book; in addition, he gave me his fascinating theory of the use of replications in the history of art quoted in this book.

An incredible intellectual climax occurred while I was writing the final chapter. A friend named Mike Lampert sent me quotations from a new book written by a popular columnist in the United Kingdom named Tim Harford. The quotes claimed that *replication* and *open communication* had been merged in the most important experiments ever in the 1600s!! This book and that experiment unknowingly and independently validated each other.

The author quoted as his source a prior book written by an eminent intellectual historian. I then purchased the book by the historian to verify that it was accurately quoted by the columnist. I provide the complete documentation of both books within that final chapter to give the reader confidence in its truth.

Until that discovery I had treated the two methods of replication and open communication separately. The two methods can be combined in what seems to be the most powerful necessities for establishing the truth.

A few other observations:

The reader will realize that I have taken the method of replication out of the chemistry lab in order to test the truth. I have done it in the world of literature and social sciences. This makes life more interesting but raises a new Issue: Control. One loses control of all the variables encountered in a complex world outside the laboratory. This is thought to be one of the causes of the difficulties experienced in the field of Psychology discussed later in the book. But it did work in examples I report in this book. I think we need an additional criterion for truth in such areas, the need for the truth seeker in these areas to have a wholistic knowledge of the case as well as purity of motives, keeping total honesty as the highest criterion.

Replications and communication can both fail to work, but the former can do so and still reveal the truth. Readers will perhaps find some failures more interesting and educational than successes. My first experience with replication taught me that it could either reveal a false or a positive truth. The failure itself provides us with a negative truth. We can learn that a theory or its hypothesis was not true as tested. That may call for, or demand, other hypotheses to explain *why* the replication failed.

What will the reader get from this book? I make bold to claim that she or he will read about some fascinating cases yielding us the truth, positive and negative. Readers will also learn about methods that they can apply that will make their professional, organizational, and private life more confident and secure. For example, is it wise to seek a second medical opinion after a painful first opinion? Is it not wise to get at least two estimates from different sources before making any major purchase?

William Empson gave us the idea that a book could have two plots, or subplots. I was inspired by him to provide three subplots within this book that the reader will encounter. They are introduced in this order: Replication, first; Open Communication, second; and throughout the third subplot is the excitement of participating in an academic revolution, the conversion of the single oldest academic discipline dating back to Aristotle, in Ancient Greece, called Rhetoric; it was called the field of Speech when I entered the academic world, and I was able to participate in making it into a new discipline of the Twenty-First Century: Communication. Get ready for the ride.

Procedural Note: Rather than footnotes and bibliography, I have provided enough documentation in the text for readers to find my bibliographic sources. If this or anything else is a problem for a reader, please let me know at Tompkinp@Colorado.Edu.

Chapter One
My First Faculty Meeting

I was a bit nervous when I rose in our modest rental house in Lafayette, Indiana, on a beautiful morning in the early fall of 1962. I was 29, White, about five feet eight inches tall, 175 pounds of bone and muscle. I had a bit of breakfast after brushing, combing, shaving and dressing. I got in the car to drive across the "Dear Dirty Wabash," the river dividing Lafayette and West Lafayette, Indiana, the latter being the home of Purdue University. I parked on campus and walked a short way to my small office in Heavilon Hall, the home of the Departments of Speech and English. Our Speech department was one of the largest in the country if not the world because the huge Engineering Schools at Purdue required all their students to take Speech 114, the introductory course. The Department of Speech, later to become the Lamb School of Communication, was located administratively in the School of Humanities, Social Science, and Education—the acronym was pronounced "Hissy"—also a source of many students taking that basic course.

Dropping my briefcase in my small office, I grabbed a pad and pen for notes I would be taking in my first faculty meeting as an Assistant Professor, the beginner's rank on the faculty tenure track. I did not see any colleagues preparing to leave so I walked by myself west from Heavilon Hall to the street where I turned right, north, to the largest auditorium in the world: The Hall of Music. I am not sure how many seats it contained, but we knew it was the biggest because Purdue's internal Public Relations personnel regularly reminded us.

I was one of the first to arrive for the meeting. My nervousness increased because of the pressure created by the fact that this was *not* a meeting of my department, not even my school or college, but of the *entire* university faculty. I had received my Ph.D. degree in the previous spring term. After an interval I started looking for a job and received an offer from the California State University System. I also had an offer from the Chrysler Corporation because my degree and training were in the brand-new field of Organizational Communication, or the analysis of complex organizations as communication systems. Their offer was $22,000 a year, plus a new free car every six months. The challenge was to create a new job in charge of Upward-Directed Communication. I did not like the idea that this position would put me in a rivalry with the United Auto Workers. They believed their most important function was to represent the workers to management. While I was considering these offers, the Head of the Department of Speech at Purdue, Alan H. Monroe, called me into his huge office in Heavilon. He got to the point without introduction: "We are offering you a position as Assistant Professor of Speech for a salary of $7,200 a year and Purdue will pay all of your retirement fees to TIAA." I was so stunned that it took me several days to say "yes" to the offer to let me continue as a Boilermaker.

I took a seat as near to the stage as I could get, in the third row. I looked around and saw none of my colleagues from Speech. *Why? I wondered.* I had heard some senior professors say that it was highly unusual to have a university-wide faculty meeting without also having received an agenda of the main business items in advance. When the time arrived, a man I recognized took the center of the stage. I had dealt with him when I was a graduate student; he was the Dean of the Graduate School. In relating this most memorable experience, I must mention that Alan H. Monroe, the Head of the Department of Speech who offered me the job, had become famous for writing a textbook, *Principles and Types of Speech*. It was used as the textbook in Speech 114 at Purdue, and in courses at many other colleges and universities. It must have brought in a fortune in royalties. It featured an organizing scheme called the Motivated Sequence with five steps for persuasive speeches and three for informative talks:

1. Attention
2. Need
3. Satisfaction
4. Visualization
5. Action

It unfolded naturally as the meeting proceeded. The Graduate School Dean delivered a captivating Attention Step: "This is the saddest day of my career." *What could be that sad?* I asked myself.

He made it possible for someone else to develop the Need or problem Step, doing so by calling on the Head of the Chemistry Department, the biggest one on campus located in a huge building next to Heavilon Hall. The Head seemed a bit embarrassed as he introduced his Satisfaction Step before the Need Step. He did this by offering a motion to the faculty *to rescind a Ph.D. degree* from one of their former students. The audience was hushed, silent, then gradually became audibly and visibly restless as the motion was seconded. *I will have to vote on whether to take away a doctoral degree?!*

The Head of Chemistry then began the narration of his Need Step, or problem to be solved. They had a graduate student who had worked with one of their internationally famous professors who had a well-known research program in which experiments—including student dissertations—were designed to build upon the findings of previous studies. The student in question had a reputation for being highly intelligent. He proposed a laboratory study that was approved by his dissertation committee of Chemistry professors. After the usual time period he presented his findings to the committee in the form of a doctoral dissertation. It was approved and the student then accepted a prestigious postdoctoral appointment in the Chemistry Department at the University of Chicago.

The narrative continued with the next graduate student in line. When he began his dissertation research, one designed to build upon the findings of the former student, his first results did not make sense. He tried again without success. The professor then directed the student to *replicate*, or repeat exactly, the experiments reported by the previous student. He followed instructions exactly but did *not* get the same results as reported in the previous student's dissertation.

The Chemistry Head said they invited the former student, now at the University of Chicago, to return to Purdue to discuss the problem. The former student, who had accepted an offer to move on from the University of Chicago to a position at the State University of Iowa, declined to accept the invitation. Purdue's Chemistry Department did some historical research on the student, finding that the missing year on his Curriculum Vitae, or academic resume', was due to the finding that he had been expelled from an Ivy League University for a lesser but similar offense. Faculty members looked at the lab analyst's reports for the dissertation in question. It was explained to the non-chemists among us that at the end of each research session in the lab, each researcher was required to submit his or her findings to an official lab analyst who would analyze and then record the chemical findings. The student in question was found to have *forged* his lab analysts' reports. They also found that after being informed of the failure and his having declined the invitation to come back for a visit to Purdue, he made a telephone call to the Registrar's Office to get transcripts, presumably to have proof he had once earned a doctorate.

The collateral evidence supported the claim that he was guilty of fabricating his data. An observation of considerable interest was made by the chemistry professors involved in the expose: one was quoted as saying it took far greater intelligence and creativity to *invent* a complex, coherent, and persuasive set of data than to report simply what was in in a lab analyst's report. *What would happen to such creativity if we ended his career as chemist?*

At this point I was nearly knocked out of my seat by the revelation that the faculty in the Chemistry Department felt that it took a high level of knowledge and imagination for the student to have *created* that fictitious yet persuasive set of findings. I moved into the Visualization Step. He was finished at the U. of Chicago and would lose the job at the State University of Iowa.

The case has haunted me ever since. What happened to the young man? Was he ever able to recover from this fall, to use that intelligence and creativity in a pro-social way? I have assumed over the years that he *may* have derived some satisfaction from fooling an audience the way playwrights, directors, and actors do. Finally, I wondered whether he considered the possibility of his creation being *replicated*. If not, he was not so brilliant as I had first assumed.

There was not a long discussion of the motion. We effected our own individual Visualization Step by projecting into the future, by the vision of the young man being stripped of his degree and losing his appointment at the State University of Iowa. Before taking the Action Step, voting on the motion to rescind, a member of the Physics Department expressed his anger about this travesty, articulating the charge that the big Chemistry Department was not exercising effective surveillance and control over its graduate students. It is only now, more than a half century removed, that I have come to realize while composing this chapter that the topic of organizational *control* would become an important topic in my later studies of organizational communication. Was there an unconscious, but powerful connection to this unique academic meeting and our action?

I remember nothing about the rest of the day except that I went over and over this gripping and depressing academic drama, over time moving it into my permanent memory by relating it to colleagues and students. It has remained vivid and important to me ever since. I thought that it would be difficult to replicate dissertations in say, English, Speech and Psychology. I would study the various means of that complex word, *replication*, and find its use in important situations. I hoped that I could find situations in the humanities and social sciences where replication as proof could be powerfully employed. Later I would come to accept another person's division of replications into two categories: Exact and Conceptual.

Although I had not yet discovered the phenomenon of Open Communication, I can see now that the Chemistry Department practiced it in conducting the dissertation replication, and in bringing it to the Graduate School and ultimately the entire faculty. I would not have learned about the power of replication that day without open communication.

And although I saw the power of replication as a method of finding the truth, in this case the chemists had to supply rhetorical explanations of *why* the replication failed: the former student purposely faked the data.

Chapter Two
Coming to Know Kenneth Burke

My life entered a new drama during that first year on the faculty of Purdue University, 1962-63, by the actions of the graduate students in our department. While still a student myself the year before I had organized the graduate students into a group called the "Non Sequiturs." Our motto, "We do not necessarily follow," a shorthand slogan *of the fallacy it defines*. We pretended to be a kind of labor union for the lowest workers in the academic line of command. It was a funny way of reminding the faculty and administration that our field, Rhetoric, originated among the Ancient Greeks because they were experimenting with democracy. We should all be prepared to make arguments and evaluate them. We should listen to the claims of all people in the system.

The Non Sequiturs had gone their own way after I moved up from the student ranks to that of faculty. I was as surprised as anyone when they, the Non Sequiturs, announced that they had invited Kenneth Burke to speak to the Department during the next semester. *The* Kenneth Burke! It was a name I knew well but about his work I knew little. No courses had been available to me and I knew that his visit would motivate me to take a crash course in his huge body of work, volumes of books published by Prentice-Hall and later the University of California Press. But when the graduate students announced his acceptance, they admitted they had no money to offer him. That meant that the Department had to come to their financial rescue. The money was found, of course, and the visit went forward.

I was greatly honored to be selected to be Burke's guide on campus during his visit. I picked him up in the hotel located in the Student Center on campus, take him to Heavilon Hall for class-room visits, speeches, coffee and then back home at night. He sought my conversation when I picked him up and took him to the appointments. One of those small group sessions was in a classroom. There was a man in the English Department who was more than a bit of a bully. The Speech and English Departments shared Heavilon Hall, including a lunchroom on the third floor. There was not a lot of communication between the two groups. We felt they looked down on us because we weren't teaching the classics of written literature, but instead thinking of us as merely studying and teaching Elocution. We sat at different tables having coffee and lunch, but there was a man in the English Department whose presence was palpable:

He was, as mentioned above, a bit of a bully. We could hear him bullying his colleagues from time to time.

Sure enough, he was in the front row in a meeting to be held in a Heavilon Hall classroom. I brought Burke over, gave him a chair in front of the room and turned to the group. I had asked him about how he wanted me to introduce him. I told the audience he had no earned degrees but had received a number of honorary doctorates from Ivy League schools and other institutions of higher education. He had written a long list of books, too many to mention. Finally, I drew back the curtain and said:

"Here is Kenneth Burke."

People were quite respectful, even deferential to this great theoretical scholar in their questioning. Then the bully began to ask questions and make the point he disagreed with Burke about Aristotle's *Poetics.*

"Oh," said Burke in a calm way, "You are quoting the so-and-so translation. Here it is in the original Greek: . . ." He spoke the ancient Greek words. Then he translated the Greek passage into English in a way that no one was able to question. It was the perfect putdown. My respect for KB, as he asked me to refer to him in conversation, grew with each of his monologues. I began asking questions about his theories, basic question my students would ask of me.

"Is your theory of Dramatism more than a metaphor?"

"Yes, people do literally act."

"But 'act' has two meanings, at least."

"Yes, as I have written, 'things move, people act.' The Stimulus-Response in Behaviorist Psychology is much too simple. We do decide to act. And, yes, we are aware that we are 'acting before an audience.' We rehearse in our mind what we will do and say when others are there to observe and listen."

I listened with fascination, later making notes about what he said and how I interpreted it. He was even open to talk about the personal side of his life. For example, one morning I met him in the Union for breakfast. He talked about his insomnia and how he listened to the radio in his room much of the night, later quoting some of the strange things he heard. I had been told he was a heavy drinker.

"Do you ever take a drink to go to sleep?"

"No," he replied, "not while trying to sleep. I learned a long time ago that a drink while trying to get to sleep becomes a stimulus—the kind that does give you a biological response. It also makes me want another drink."

His public lecture attracted one of the largest audiences I ever saw at Purdue or any other university. Every faculty member from the Humanities must have been there—and I recognized many from the Social Sciences. One of the graduate students from the Non Sequiturs introduced Burke for this major lecture. The title of his lecture was "On the Suasive Nature of Even the Ordinary Nomenclatures." He established that language itself has a rhetorical nature. I memorized the title and some of the main points. Several years later, in 1966, the lecture he gave appeared as a chapter with a new title: "Terministic Screens," in a new and important book: *Language as Symbolic Action: Essays on Life, Literature, and Method.* A key sentence printed as a paragraph in the essay sounded familiar:

> Even if any given terminology is a *reflection* of reality, by its very
> nature as a terminology it must be a *selection* of reality; and to this
> *extent it must function also as a deflection* of reality. (p. 45).

I was privately proud that our Department, our graduate students had invited him and presented him to a huge audience. In addition, he demonstrated that our rhetorical approach to language is the basic or primary one, even for the top literary critic of his age.

Our conversations were fascinating to me. I have recalled them and have added details picked up in conversation at later times. One of our most revealing conversations came when I asked him how he could have received a bunch of honorary degrees from Yale and Harvard without having even an undergraduate degree.

"How?"

"I spent a freshman year at Ohio State University and was disappointed because I couldn't get into the advanced and graduate classes. So, at the end of the year I made my dad an offer: 'give me what you spent this past year while I live in New York, in Greenwich Village. I promise I will study hard and learn more.' He agreed."

KB then told me about living in Greenwich Village. I think he said E. E. Cummings, poet, painter, author, was his roommate for part of the time. I remember distinctly hearing him talk about Prohibition during the 1920s.

"They put poison in the alcohol, but we drank it anyway. Oh, we had terrible hangovers."

"What about the *Dial*? What did you do there, an avant-garde literary magazine?"

"I did any job they needed for a while. I wrote music reviews. But one day the boss said to a group of us, 'there is this great German author whose work they rave about in Europe. I wish we had something of his translated into English. I would publish it in the *Dial*. His name is Thomas Mann.'"

"The next day I brought in my translation of *Death in Venice*. They all thought I had translated it overnight. I explained that while at Ohio State I had met a German professor who informed me what contemporary works I should read. I read *Death in Venice* in German and translated it for the professor. It was then published in the *Dial*."

Later I read the novella, about the adult man's preoccupation with the fourteen-year-old boy's beauty in Venice. Phil Tompkins was not, and is still not, unimpressed.

I would have many more meetings with KB. A letter from him is reproduced later in this book. A theory of Organizational Identification drawn from his work will also be mentioned in a subsequent chapter. No single theorist ever influenced my life as much as Kenneth Burke.

Chapter Three
Moving on from Purdue

Of the two categories of replications, illustrated by the chemistry case was, of course, Exact replication. In that case it was the failure to replicate results. I memorized the event by reviewing it over and over, relating it to students in my classes when we were faced with how we come to know, what we come to know as the *truth,* or what the Philosophers call the study of Epistemology. That topic comes up constantly in communication courses because of the field's history. Speech has now been mainly modernized and expanded by changing its name to Communication, but it has and should continue to remember its history as the *first* academic discipline in ancient Greece: Rhetoric. Yes, the word has come to have a negative connotation, but that is because of being often used as applying only to ignorant, bigoted, and fallacious discourse. Classical Rhetoric prepared human beings to argue logically with examples as induction and the enthymeme as the first deductive form of reasoning.

I was a member of the debate and wrestling teams at Wichita North High School and later at what is now the University of Northern Colorado, taking courses in logic and rhetoric. One team was all about using brains, the other using brawn with our brains. To this day I think Aristotle's *Rhetoric* is an amazing document.

Some readers might be wondering, what does rhetoric or persuasion have to do with the truth? In many cases, I venture to claim, it is necessary to persuade audiences to accept the truth. Scientific audiences may have higher and tighter criteria than the listeners of a politician; nonetheless, recall that the faculty dissertation committee members at Purdue, all scientists, were persuaded to accept the completely *fictitious* findings as the truth, persuaded to sign the document, accepting it as true. Recall that in arguing in favor of rescinding the doctoral degree they provided us with circumstantial evidence of guilt in order to persuade us to vote their way. The doctoral committee must have believed the student had ethos or credibility, a logical set of data, and emotional proof might have been the appreciation of the dissertation's appearance of "wholeness."

A Definition of Epistemology

After a couple of friends who read the first draft of this book said I needed to revise this section, I looked for a definition of *epistemology*. A dictionary of philosophy had pages and pages of discourse about this word, but Google said simply his. Epistemology is "the theory of knowledge, especially with regard to its methods, validity, and scope. Epistemology is the investigation of what distinguishes justified belief from opinion." I like several things about it. The word *methods*, for example, is in the title of this book. In addition, I am seeking the kind of truth-seeking methods that are practical in nature.

Notice that the faculty at Purdue had to be persuaded of a negative truth. The dissertation was false, but a deceptive one. The method of replication did not alone make that a justified belief. It was the apparently true statements about forging lab tests, the rhetorical arguments that did so. The chemists probably did not know that rhetoric as a discipline came before chemistry. But it took rhetoric to produce the persuasive power of their replication.

It was exciting to bring classical rhetoric into modern organizational and management theory. Don't managers of organizations try to persuade us of many things? As a new Assistant Professor, I was given the job of creating the first undergraduate courses in Organizational Communication at Purdue. My doctoral advisor, W. Charles Redding, was the major founder of the new field; he had recruited me to Purdue, treated me as an important graduate student, but had poured all his time and energy into the graduate courses and seminars. He was grateful that I was translating his and others' work into syllabi, or course outlines, for Purdue's undergraduate students. He accepted me as a colleague and helped me whenever I asked.

I was also doing research and publishing at a rate that would guarantee promotion to Associate Professor with Tenure within three years. And I now carried with me that concept of Replication. It gave me a sense of respect for the sciences, including Chemistry of course, because they could make exact replications of studies using an independent laboratory analyst at the end of the day, or night, to attest to the validity of the chemicals claimed to be obtained. I had a case of envy to tell the truth, but Phil Tompkins was driven by the excitement of using the Greek tradition with the insights and methods of modern social science to make this new field of Communication exciting and capable of achieving the truth.

Teaching Barnard's Executive Functions

It was easy for me to decide what would come first in my undergraduate courses: a summary of a book published in 1938 by the Harvard University Press: *The Functions of the Executive*, by Chester I. Barnard, a successful executive himself. Let me quote the three executive functions task managers must perform, and then elaborate them: "(1) communication; (2) willingness to serve; (3) common purpose." Read them again and test this interpretation: they are all about communication, a good way to emphasize to students the a, b, cs of Organizational Communication.

The first function is to establish the communication system, the channels, tying all members together. The organization chart is an attempt to represent it graphically, except *informal* channels. A line or channel must reach every person coming down the line and going back up.

The second function is also communicative in nature. Creating the willingness of persons to serve must include communication reaching out to recruit members. That recruiting must continue so long as the organization exists, figuring out the *persuasive* inducements to offer recruits. Another process is that of offering inducements—raises, for example--to keep them happy working in the organization.

The third function, again, is all about communication. How can we know our common purposes unless an executive articulates and communicates common purposes, including the jobs from the bottom to the top, the lower and the higher positions within the hierarchy or structure of positions from the top to the base of the triangle, the shape of the channels forming the graphic organization chart.

I also talked to undergraduates about the work of Nobel Laureate Herbert A. Simon, whose work was influenced by Barnard. The Nobel Committee said they could have used Simon's theories of decision making in making the decision to give him the prize. In 1985 Robert D. McPhee and I edited a book with this title: *Organizational Communication: Traditional Themes and New Directions*. It includes a chapter by Phillip K. Tompkins and George Cheney, a former graduate student of mine. The title is: "Communication and Unobtrusive Control in Contemporary Organizations."

In it we say one of the Nobel Laureate's ideas was that companies and other organizations provided their workers with the *premises* of deductive decisions they would make about specifics every day. In our book chapter we used my example: Aristotle spoke of the enthymeme as a deductive rhetorical argument in which the speaker drew from societal beliefs—in the head of listeners—the premises from which to draw their audiences to the desired conclusion. I called Aristotle's deductive argument, using the premises in the mind of audiences, as Enthymeme I and Simon's corporate example Enthymeme 2. That is, rather than depending on society to implant premises in the memory of the company's recruits, managers implant the specific, desired decision premises. I developed a pun to illustrate: Management says "Use these premises when on our premises."

To make this less abstract, in Chapter Six I will explicitly identify the main decisional premises Dr. Wernher von Braun and his associates impressed on the memory of every technical civil servant of NASA's Marshall Space Center. I will also mention some alternatives that a Bureaucrat in Washington tried to impose on the Space Center, without much success—thankfully.

It was exciting to work at the source, Purdue University, of the emergence of our new field of study. Yes, it was still a Department of Speech, but Professor Redding had also been one of the founders of a new professional organization for us in the revolution, the National Society for the Study of Communication, NSSC. Later it would change its name to the International Communication Association, the ICA. There were some drawbacks as well as attractions for me at Purdue: for example, Redding taught all the graduate courses, which is the way it should have been, even though I yearned for the opportunity to teach some of them. Then in 1965 my wife divorced me just before an invitation to interview for a job at the Department of Speech at Wayne State University in Detroit, Michigan.

Job Interview

The interview went better than I expected. I made a good connection with a young man my age, Edward J. Pappas; we would become close friends, a brotherly relationship. Wayne State University is in the center of a major city and I enjoyed the urban atmosphere. I had turned down the offer from Chrysler three years earlier that would have brought me to that area. I also wanted my own baseball team—wanted one to *identify* with, to root for. So, part of the offer was from the Detroit Tigers. (Just kidding of course.) The offer came in soon after my visit and it was a promotion to Associate Professor with tenure and, of course, a raise in salary. I accepted it. It would be my home base and I would make a couple of trips around the bases while with the Tigers.

Before I move us to WSU and Detroit, the reader needs to know how I came to be at Purdue as a graduate student and Assistant Professor. Upon graduating in 1956 from the Speech Department at the University of Northern Colorado, I accepted the offer of an assistantship for the fall term at the University of Nebraska. I was influenced by a young and extraordinary faculty member named H. Bruce Kendall, who was still working on his doctorate at the University of Wisconsin. He chided me, hurting my feelings, by criticizing my writing in an essay I showed him. I studied style books and learned a lot, including that careful re-writing was a good way for me to achieve a well-written document. I wrote my M.A. thesis, the title of which is "George W. Norris's Persuasion in the Campaign for the Unicameral Legislature." Bruce had suggested several problems I could check out in the library as topics to consider; Norris and the Unicameral constituted my choice: On November 6, 1934, the people of Nebraska changed, by amendment to their state constitution, from a bicameral to a unicameral or one-house legislature of between thirty and fifty members to be elected on a nonpartisan basis. The unicameral legislature stands today without Republicans and Democrats. How did it happen? My thesis submitted that it happened by the single-handed campaign of the senior U.S. Senator of the state named George W. Norris. Norris was a super star of his age, politically speaking. First elected as a Republican, he later became an Independent. He sponsored the Tennessee Valley Authority, or TVA, legislation and became one of the stars in the book, *Profiles in Courage*, written by a young Democratic Senator from Massachusetts named John F. Kennedy.

Kennedy also chaired a Senate Committee to select members for the Senate Hall of Fame. Norris was not selected. I wrote to Senator Kennedy about my thesis research and asked why Senator Norris was not chosen. I got a letter back from Senator Kennedy, no doubt because one of his speech writers and aides, Ted Sorenson, was from Nebraska, and whose father C.A. Sorenson, served as Attorney General of Nebraska from 1929 to 1933, and was a friend of Senator Norris. The letter from Kennedy explained that a Republican member of the Selection Committee had served with Norris in the Senate and could not vote for him. (That Christmas, 1956, I also received a card from Kennedy that I still treasure, including a color photograph of him, Jackie and their daughter Caroline Kennedy.)

Norris travelled from city to city to advocate the Unicameral Non-Partisan Legislature. I followed him twenty some years later by reading local newspaper coverage of his speeches. Norris gave logical arguments, enthymemes, about the dirty politics conducted in secrecy that went on in the Conference Committees of the U.S. Legislature that had to reach agreement about different versions of the same legislation passed by both the House and Senate. But he asked the voters in every speech to do it because *he*, George Norris, was supporting it. He told the large audiences that they knew he could be trusted to argue for the right cause. He made it a matter of Ethos, as Aristotle called it, his personal credibility.

While working on the M.A. thesis I was still thinking that I should enter law school so that I could use my debating skills as an attorney at law, but I had much enjoyed helping teach speech and debate classes as part of my assistantship; I also enjoyed doing my thesis research. So, Bruce Kendall helped me with my conflict by getting an offer for me from the Department of Speech and Drama, at the University of Kansas at Lawrence, as an Instructor of Speech and Assistant Debate Coach for $3,200 a year on the beautiful Mount Oread campus in the middle of Lawrence, Kansas. The other Instructor and Assistant Debate Coach, Wilmer A. Linkugel, also a former M.A. student of Bruce Kendall's, would become one of my closest, brotherlike friends until his death a few years ago.

I loved teaching on that beautiful campus. I had an office for the first year in the basement of the Law School, but lost interest in becoming an attorney. *Where could I find better clients or customers than in the classroom of a university?* Dr. William "Bill" Conboy, our young and bright Department Chair told me of a new Ph.D. program that was part of the revolution to expand the field into one of Communication. He also persuaded me to investigate the program being developed by Professor W. Charles Redding at Purdue University.

Let me reassure the reader that this book is neither an autobiography nor a memoir. It is a collection of stories about the learning of methods to find the truth. It is necessary, however, to slip in autobiographical details that permitted me to be *in the right place* or *situation* at the *right time* to discover the truth about learning the truth. For example, two unconnected events occurred while I was teaching at KU that later helped me gain an important set of truths. The two events happened in November of 1958 and November of 1959.

Lowell Lee Andrews Case

The first involved a sophomore student named Lowell Lee Andrews, who had taken Speech I from me at KU, as a tall, heavy set young man with a baby face and spectacles who went home to Wolcott, Kansas during KU's Thanksgiving break and killed his sister, mother, and father. He tried to make it look like a burglary-murder before going back to Lawrence to attend a movie, *Mardi Gras*, at the Granada Movie Theater where he got a ticket stub to serve as an alibi. He went back home, called the police to report his findings. They became suspicious of the absence of any observable emotional response to the deaths of the three members of his family. They brought in the family minister who got Lowell to talk and eventually confess. His motive was explained by a desire to use the family's money to buy a new car and become a hit man in a big city. This forced me to rerun in my mind his speeches and participation in class discussions. He was extremely quiet and gave his speeches without observable emotion or conviction. I could not have predicted his later actions.

The Clutter Murders

The other incident occurred while I was a student at Purdue after the two years of teaching at KU. It happened in the tiny town of Holcomb, Kansas—again in my home state—on November 15, 1959. Four members of the distinguished Clutter family were found bound and shot to death in their home: Husband and father, Herbert Clutter; wife and mother, Bonnie, daughter Nancy, and son Kenyon. National attention was given to the case, partly because Herbert had served in the Eisenhower Administration. Unknown to me at the time, the New York *Times* article about the case caught the attention of a short-story writer and novelist living in New York city. It caught my attention also because I had passed through and stopped in Garden City, Kansas, close to Holcomb. I was now studying for a doctoral degree in West Lafayette, Indiana, so far away in miles but so close in my consciousness and identifications. What I could *not* foresee was that the two cases—Lowell Lee Andrews and the Clutter case—would merge, requiring research and literary-rhetorical criticism from me because of what was at stake: *The Truth and the Method of Learning It.*

I got a cheap apartment in Detroit because Wayne State University is an urban university, located in the heart of downtown Detroit. Our department was temporarily housed in two old two-story houses, while waiting to occupy a new building. My office was in an upstairs bedroom of a house on the edge of campus. I walked to other buildings to meet classes and quickly came to respect those WSU students more than any I had known before because of their extra effort. Many of my classes, even undergraduate ones, were taught at night to facilitate the many students with jobs. Many of the students did have jobs and read their textbooks, say, during a bus ride from work to campus and back home. They were older than the other students I had worked with at KU and Purdue and their real-world experiences allowed them to help me teach classes in organizational communication.

Another feature I enjoyed was getting to meet people in other departments. I met a couple in the English Department who got me reading the magical prose of James Joyce, perhaps the greatest prose writer in history. The *Dubliners,* for example, is a book of short stories I devoured in one afternoon, and then began to use one of the stories to help me teach organizational communication classes, letting the drama of the tale show how the hierarchical discourse at the place of work can affect our actions at home at the end of the day. Here is a terse summary of that story Joyce called "Counterparts."

Farrington is ordered up to the office of the boss, Mr. Alleyne, who asks why he must again complain about Farrington's work. Why hadn't he made a copy of the new contract? Alleyne continues to humiliate him in a stream of harsh words in front of a woman, a stranger to Farrington. The abuse makes him becomes furious, giving him an urge to do harm to Alleyne but instead goes back to work. Frustrated by the work of copying, he gets thirsty, persuades himself to have a drink or two before he finishes the work. He buys a round for drinkers in the pub, a round leads to another, and then he is humiliated again by running out of money and must go home rather drunk. His son, a subordinate in the familial hierarchy, has let the fire die out so Farrington begins to beat the boy. The line that lowers the curtain on the drama is:

"Oh, pa . . . I'll say a Hail Mary if you don't beat me . . . ."

Chapter Four
Finding the Truth

Sometime during 1965 I visited my erstwhile mentor, Bruce Kendall, a bachelor living in West Lafayette. He had guided my M.A. work and then got me a job at the University of Kansas. After I was promoted to the faculty at Purdue, I nominated him for the job of administering the huge basic course, Speech 114. He had, of course, finished his Ph.D. before moving to Purdue.

After a catchup conversation, he put some Debussy on the turntable and presented me with a martini and a copy of the *New Yorker* magazine opened to something serialized about my home state of Kansas. It was by Truman Capote and the title was "In Cold Blood." It was about *the* Clutter Case, the murders of each member of a family of four in western Kansas that I had read about first in 1959 and later. I gave it my speed-reading treatment, got the second installment and a second martini from Bruce. After I finished those first and second parts, we talked about them. Bruce thought they were brilliant and wanted me, his mentee from Kansas, to agree with him. I thought it was written well, compelling, yet I noted that the author had made some minor factual errors in it. I would withhold judgment until I had avidly but carefully read the final two parts. I looked forward to finishing *ICB* when I got home.

When I returned to my apartment in Detroit, I feverishly read the last two installments and bought the book, *In Cold Blood,* as soon as it was published, during its early life of fantastic fanfare and runaway sales. Nearly every major magazine reviewed it early, almost all in a positive way. I found some more minor errors of fact and interpretation. Capote had not understood the strange history of liquor laws in Kansas. And then—there was Lowell Lee Andrews as a character in the book! Yes, my former student, Lowell Lee Andrews, appears as a character in the work. I was magnetized. He was on death row with the two Clutter killers, Richard Hickock and Perry Smith, at the penitentiary in Kansas. The character as portrayed by Capote, however, was not exactly the young man I knew. Capote's Andrews was much more brilliantly intelligent and naturally outgoing than the student I had in Speech 1 at KU and still remembered well.

The factual accuracy of the book had become a much bigger issue than in my conversation with Bruce because of the author's incessant promotion of the book with journalists and reviewers. He said that it was *true, every word of it,* and that it was a new literary genre, the nonfiction novel. *Hmm,* I thought, *if that is so it will require a new genre of literary criticism: Rhetorical-Literary Criticism,* which unlike traditional literary criticism, takes serious account of a work's factual accuracy.

As I read what the reviewers had to say in the top magazines and newspapers it became clear that they did not know how to handle this new genre, this nonfiction novel. Some realized that accuracy was important and yet did not know how to treat it; one assumed it to be true on the basis of "Internal evidence." That still makes no sense to me. The famous literary theorist and critic, Kenneth Burke, wrote that every living thing is a critic, or it would not long be a living thing. Even a trout must learn to discriminate or distinguish between a *real* and an *artificial* fly. I was beginning to lose a bit of faith in the author and the reviewers who took the book to be true because the author claimed it to be so.

A Formal Exchange of Messages

I decided to write to him in care of Random House, the book's publisher. Before me now is the thin sheet of yellow paper used in those days to make carbon copies, which means one of the department secretaries typed it for me:

January 19, 1966

Dear Mr. Capote:

I am working on a book about you and In Cold Blood [underlined]. Although I shall continue under any conditions, it would be most helpful if I could get your approval and cooperation. It seems to me that the theory and history of such literary innovation should be recorded as soon (and accurately) as possible. What makes me qualified to write this book? (1) I am a native Kansan, know that country and its people well; (2) Lowell Lee Andrews was a student of mine at the University of Kansas; (3) I followed the Clutter case, and have talked with close friends who live in the Garden City area about the case and its impact on their lives; (4) I have professional interest in interpersonal communication—your data-gathering methods (i.e., the interviewing techniques) appear to be just as revolutionary as the literary form of In Cold Blood [underlined]; and (5) I have a lively interest in literature (and have an amateur's interest in criticism).

What am I asking of you? Suggest a convenient time and I'll drop everything, come to New York and bombard you with questions. Unfortunately, I shall have to take notes!

Please consider this seriously. If you take In Cold Blood [underlined] as seriously as I do, you will want to preserve the literary rationale and methodology of the work for future readers, critics, and writers.

If you are neither interested nor able to help me, please wire, call or write me a "no," so that I shall know that you don't want to be bothered by further requests.

Sincerely,

Phillip K. Tompkins

Associate Professor

The comment about the manner of interviewing was an allusion to the widespread reporting that Capote did not have to take notes. He could remember exactly every word of an interviewee's answers, or so he had claimed in many interviews.

One week later I received a letter postmarked Bridgehampton, N.Y. on January 26, 1966. It was addressed to P.K. Tompkins, Esq., West Grand Blvd., Detroit 2, Michigan. There was a printed message on the outside of the folded card I took out of the envelope. I reproduce it here:

Of the first edition of
IN COLD BLOOD
five hundred copies have been printed on
special paper and specially bound.
Each copy is signed by the author and numbered.

A large X in blue ink had been drawn through this message, lest I come to think I was going to receive a signed, numbered copy of the hot book. No, I would not be receiving a signed copy on special paper with a special binding. I opened the card and found a handwritten note. Here are the words and the spacing the author used:

Dear Mr. Tomkins [sic]—
To judge from my
mail, a good dozen critics plan
books along
this order. But of course
you have my blessings, and I wish
you all the luck in the world. As
for my personally cooperating—the
truth is this: I am working on
a new book, simply can't let
anything else interfere with my
already harassed energies (600
letters a day!), and I am going

abroad next week to save my
sanity. But believe me, all
good wishes—

T. Capote

I would have to go to Kansas to learn the truth without his help. I arranged for my classes to be covered for the few days I would be gone. I got in my car on February 4, 1966, a cold and snowy day in Detroit, and headed south and west for a nine-day trip to Kansas. I first stopped in Wichita to see my mother, other family members and get a good night's sleep. The next day I drove to Garden City, Kansas and by chance checked into the same motel where Capote stayed. Everyone, it seemed, wanted to tell me about "them."

"Them?"

"Yes, Truman and Nelle, his friend."

They were eager to tell me that he was short and effeminate, she tall and masculine. They also weakened Capote's claim to have a near-perfect memory. Nelle was said to sit in on many of his interviews and took copious notes of what was said by the interviewees. It took me some time to realize that Nelle was better known as Harper Lee, Capote's childhood friend and the author of *To Kill a Mockingbird*. She had come with him to help with interviews and observations.

My best decision, bordering on prescience, was to go directly to the Garden City *Telegram*, where I was immediately welcomed by the Editor, Bill Brown; he could not have been more helpful to a young researcher. He said he would provide me with key information—after he sat me down to read the back files of his newspaper and those of the Hutchinson *News* for the days in which the mass murders were reported. Later editions reported the trial in the Finney County Courthouse. After I had a gestalt, a whole view of the actions within the story, Editor Brown gave me a standup interview in which he told me about Perry Smith's speech at the gallows, and what Smith did *not* say that Capote put in the book. Brown said that he took notes and compared them with the other reporters who also took notes. They agreed exactly upon what was said: Is replication in reporting not verification, the truth?

While reading the newspaper files I was surprised to discover that the central figure in the case gets little notice in *In Cold Blood*: that role was almost completely diminished! His name is Duane West, then the Finney County Attorney who was totally involved in the case from the time the murder victims were discovered until he completed the prosecution of the two suspects, and his legal responsibilities were completed. My two interviews with Duane West provided me with the most important and persuasive facts I would later use. On the way back from Garden City

I followed a tip from Attorney West by making a stop at the Supreme Court of the State of Kansas in Topeka. There I was allowed to read the transcript of the trial in which Richard Hickock and Perry Smith were found guilty of the murders of the four members of the Clutter family. After reading the transcript I had a few pages copied to take with me.

After leaving Topeka I stopped again to stay overnight with Bruce Kendall in West Lafayette, Indiana. He sat breathless while listening to my narrative of the evidence I found in Kansas, no doubt because he loved the book so much. I finished my report; his reply was slow and studied:

"You have got something there."

His assertion was all the stronger because it was understated and given with some reluctance.

"What are you going to do with it?"

"I am going to drive home to Detroit, write it up and try to publish it."

I returned to Detroit, caught up with my classes, thanked those who covered for me and spent all my spare time writing up the evidence in a rhetorical-critical evaluation. Jimmie Trent, fellow Kansan and colleague in the Department of Speech at Wayne State University, knew about the case and questioned me to learn the facts I had gathered while back in our home state. At the end of my list of evidence he nodded and gave me my three-word title:

"In Cold Fact."

That was it. I thanked Jimmie profusely and got back to work again. As I got close to finishing the manuscript, I was looking for a place to sell it, not as the book I had mentioned to Capote in my letter, but as an article. I admired *The Atlantic Monthly* so much that I got a name off the masthead: Michael Curtis, Associate Editor, and called him on the telephone. He seemed interested in reading what I had written and asked me to send it special delivery—no email in those days. He called me back after reading it, saying he liked it so much he showed it to colleagues on the editorial staff and they agreed with him.

"One more step to take," he said, "the Editor in Chief wants to take it home with him over the weekend to read. I'll call you at the first of the week."

That was one slow weekend for me.

"Phil," he said Monday morning when I picked up the phone. "He says 'No.' The rest of us are disappointed that we won't be able to publish it."

I was crushed. Michael's enthusiasm for the piece had built up my hopeful expectation. I was about to hang up the phone when I heard Michael move on.

"But we do have a suggestion for you. *Esquire* is one of the few important magazines *not* to have reviewed the book. That might make them ready for an article like yours."

I went home that night and put on a vinyl recording of Ein Heldenleben, or "Hero's Life," by Richard Strauss. I gradually came to like Michael's suggestion more when I remembered *Esquire* had been the most encouraging of magazines to the "New Journalism" of the time: those writers seeking excellence in literary journalism. I would come to correspond with Tom Wolfe, for example, and he agreed to cooperate with my kind of work, but other projects came to claim attention of both Wolfe and Tompkins. I went out to buy a copy of *Esquire* at the newsstand. Checking a masthead again, I found the name of the Managing Editor: Byron Dobell. I called him and he said he was interested: with a serious reservation.

"We would be interested in hearing what facts Capote changed, but we would want to publish it only if you can explain *why* he changed them," said Dobell.

"I can do that because I know his rhetorical purpose."

"Great. Send it as soon as possible."

He seemed to understand me. After sending it I was able to make the transition from disappointment over the rejection to hopeful expectation and then elation experienced upon acceptance. I received word *Esquire* would be publishing it in the June 1966 issue. Dobell told me *not* to tell anyone else what was in the article because they wanted Capote to buy a copy of the magazine at the newsstand. He had also insisted that I send my research materials to the Research Editor, a young woman whose name I have unfortunately lost since then. I called her and she enthusiastically asked me to send her copies of notes taken during interviews along with the names and telephone numbers of everyone I interviewed and quoted. That I did.

Then I waited to buy the June 1966 issue of *Esquire* at the newsstand.

Chapter Five
"In Cold Fact"

As every literate American must know by now, *In Cold Blood* is the "true account of a multiple murder and its consequences." Late in 1959, four members of the Herbert W. Clutter family were bound and shot to death in Holcomb, Kansas, by Richard Eugene Hickock and Perry Edward Smith. Nearly five and a half years later, the killers were hanged; this execution allowed Truman Capote to complete the last chapter of what has become the literary sensation of the year, if not the decade. *In Cold Blood* is organized into four main parts and 86 unnumbered chapters which generally alternate between the doings in Kansas and the doings of the killers on the road. Actually, the chapters are more like short stories; many of them could stand by themselves with little or no context. For example, my favorite is chapter 54, in which Smith and Hickock pick up a pair of hitchhikers who exist on the refund money from pop bottles—the unforgettable boy named Bill, and Johnny, his gramp. The chapters are so like short stories that they end, for critic F.W. Dupee, with too-obtrusive "curtains." All together they constitute the substance of Capote's claim that he has established a new literary form: the "nonfiction novel."

The paragraph above is the exact verbal replica of the first paragraph in my *Esquire* article, "In Cold Fact," published in the June 1966 issue. This chapter is made up of either direct quotes from the article, like the paragraph above, or summaries of sections. As the Editor of *Esquire* wanted it, both Capote and Tompkins had to buy a copy of the magazine at the newsstand. A friend named Sandy took me to lunch at the Detroit Chop House the day it came out; I bought two copies of the magazine so we could both eat, read, and talk. During this luncheon while looking ahead I realized that my final paragraph was missing, another one substituted in its place that I had never seen before. I did not completely agree with the new paragraph and said so to Sandy.

After lunch I went to the phone in my office to call Byron Dobell, the top Editor at the magazine. I told him I had never seen that final paragraph before. He tried to calm me down, then went on to say that at the last minute the magazine's lawyers had read my final paragraph and decided that Capote's lawyers "could sue us for accusing Capote of mendacity." He also said Capote had sent word, a kind of threat, that he and his lawyers would be reading the article carefully.

Mendacity

I hung up with disappointment and checked my *Shorter Oxford English Dictionary* of 1956 (London: Oxford University Press) to find this definition of mendacity: "The quality of being mendacious; habitual lying or deceiving; also, a lie or falsehood." I had not used the words *mendacious*, *mendacity*, *lie*, or *falsehood* in that final paragraph, but I was not a lawyer and had no choice but to accept their professional opinion. So, in the 55 years since then I have made a point when asked to speak or discuss the article, that is, I wish to read aloud *my* final paragraph that was redacted, removed, replaced. I hasten to add that it has never been presented in print but appears in that form below.

And while preparing the manuscript for this book I discovered for the first time that four *important* paragraphs leading up to the final paragraph had also been *deleted,* with no replacements. I understood readily why they had been erased. Their importance made me decide to change my plans for this chapter. I shall present here the article, "In Cold Fact," as published by means of quotations and summaries. In addition, when we near the conclusion I will present the five original paragraphs in print for the first time. One major reason is that I want now, as then, to shower praise on the man I regard as the virtually unknown hero of the Clutter case, a man central to solving, prosecuting, and serving as the chief oral historian of the case. I will also explain why Capote distorted the facts of the case so significantly, even punishing the real hero by saying his shoes squeaked when he took steps in the Finney County courtroom.

After the introductory paragraph presented above, my next task was to raise the question, how does one evaluate a literary form? Let us begin with a definition: A novel is a "fictional prose narrative of substantial length." Capote's new form is a contradiction: "nonfiction fiction." By quoting Capote from the *Saturday Review, New Yorker*, and *New York Times Book Review,* I made it clear that he claimed that it was "true" and that he did not give in to even a "minor distortion." Thus, one must evaluate the work, quite apart from stylistic and aesthetic criteria, by asking "Is the author's account of the events, by any objective standards, true?" Answering that involves using the methods of journalism and history.

Then I tried to develop my credentials in order to boost my Aristotelian *ethos*, to enhance my credibility as a source. I mentioned growing up in Wichita and then passing through Garden City while travelling to and from college in Colorado. I mentioned teaching for two years at the University of Kansas. During one semester a minor character in Capote's tale, Lowell Lee Andrews, took a class from me. I then got to the heart of the matter, driving to Garden City to conduct interviews with surviving principals, getting in a dig at Capote's method by putting in parenthesis "(with much note-taking on my part) and a search for documentary confirmation." Then I stated the thesis: "My investigation led me to this carefully considered conclusion: Truman Capote's *In Cold Blood* contains numerous factual inaccuracies—both trivial and serious."

I was happy to write that my task had been anticipated by a reporter for the Kansas City *Star,* Robert Pearman, who published a lengthy article with some of Capote's inaccuracies on January 27, five months before mine. The inaccuracies at first seem trivial, such as the incident in which Nancy Clutter's horse named Babe was sold at an auction. Capote builds tension by the call for bids that slowly increase: "I hear fifty . . . sixty-five . . .the bidding was laggardly, nobody seemed really to want Babe, and then the man who got her, a Mennonite farmer who said he might use her for plowing, paid seventy-five dollars. As he led her out of the corral, Susan Kidwell ran forward; she raised her hand as though to say goodbye, but instead clasped it over her mouth."

Pearman's journalistic research found that the horse was sold for $182.50 to a man who bought her first, for a sentimental reason and second, because he knew that Babe was in foal with a colt. He wanted the colt and then he sold it for $250. Babe later produced two more colts for him. The new owner let the Y. M. C. A. use Babe during the summers to train children to ride. I called that a subtler, more satisfying curtain on the Clutter girl and her horse.

Pearman found many such inaccuracies, often used by Capote to provide the little ironic flourish at the end of each chapter, a curtain, making many of the chapters able to stand as a short story. Capote was well known to use *irony* in his fiction. The *Star* reporter showed that the novelist also did it in this nonfiction book. That discovery helped me by making me sensitive to the possibility of a larger, climactic irony.

The climax of *In Cold Blood* is literally and ironically the "moment of truth" in the book. Until that point the reader is unsure of just how, and by whom, the Clutter murders were committed. In the sixty-first chapter we learn that although Richard Hickcock has made a statement in the Las Vegas Police Station, blaming Perry Smith for all four of the killings, Smith had admitted only the alibi they had agreed upon, nothing more. Capote's narrative: "And although even [Kansas Bureau of Investigation agent] Duntz had forfeited his composure—and shed, along with his coat, his enigmatic drowsy dignity—the suspect seemed content and serene; he refused to budge. He'd never heard of the Clutters or Holcomb, or even Garden City."

In the sixty-third chapter (the intervening chapter is a flashback to a café in Holcomb), K.B.I. agents Dewey and Duntz, along with Smith, are in the first of a two-car caravan headed for Garden City. Smith still has not budged. The two agents try to press Smith into confessing by repeating parts of Hickock's confession, achieving no success. Agent Dewey mentions an incident in which Smith had supposedly beaten a

Negro to death.

"To Dewey's surprise," wrote Capote, "the prisoner gasps. He twists around in his seat until he can see through the rear window, the motorcade's second car, see inside it: 'The tough boy!' Turning back, he stares at the stark streak of desert highway. 'I thought it was a stunt. I didn't believe you. That Dick let fly. The tough boy! Oh, a real brass boy. Wouldn't harm the fleas of a dog.' He spits, 'I never killed any Nigger.' He spits again. 'So Dick was afraid of me? That's amusing. I'm very amused. What he don't know is, I almost shot him.'

Dewey lights two cigarettes, one for himself, one for the prisoner. 'Tell us about it, Perry'."

And Perry Smith tells in Capote's artful nonfiction.

Now let us see what really happened. I had an early interview with Duane West, the County Prosecutor who persuaded a jury to convict Hickock and Smith. He shared with me several wonderful insights into the truth, including the information that the transcript of the trial was at the Supreme Court of Kansas in the State Capital, Topeka, Kansas. I knew then I would have to stop in Topeka on my way home to Detroit. In the office of the Clerk of the Supreme Court of Kansas there is on file the official transcript of case number 2322, District Court of Finney County, Kansas: "THE STATE OF KANSAS PLAINTIFF, vs. RICHARD EUGENE HICKOCK and PERRY EDWARD SMITH, Defendants." It is a document of 515 pages, the last one of which is signed by Lillian C. Valenzuela, Certified Shorthand Reporter, Garden City, Kansas. The following exchange, between Logan Green, assistant to the County Attorney West and K.B.I agent Dewey, is taken verbatim from pages 231-233. Dewey is testifying as to the first time that Smith made a remark implicating himself in the crime:

"Q: Where was that?

A: That was at the Police Department at Las Vegas.

Q: Did he give you any information concerning the crime?

A: He did. I told Perry Smith that Hickock had given the other agents a statement and that Hickock had said they had sold the radio, the portable radio, that they had taken from Kenyon Clutter's room, that they had sold it in Mexico City. I told Smith that they were going to send an agent down there to get the radio and that before we sent this agent I wanted to know for sure that where Hickock said that radio was, that it was there. Present when I was talking to Perry Smith on this occasion was Mr. Duntz and Mr. Dye of the Kansas Bureau of Investigation. Mr. Dye told Perry Smith where Hickock had said that he sold the portable radio, and Smith said that was right.

Q: Did he give you any further information in connection with the crimes at that time?

A: No sir.

Q: Subsequent to that did you have any other conversation with him?

A: Yes. I talked to Perry Smith later that same day, which was on the 4th of January, 1960. At that time I talked to him when we were in the car en route back to Garden City.

Q: Who was in the car with you on that trip back to Garden City?

A: Smith and Mr. Duntz and myself in one car. Sheriff Robinson and Mr. Church, of the Kansas Bureau of Investigation, and Hickock were in the other car.

Q: On the way back you say he gave you some additional information?

A: He did.

Q: I will ask you to tell the Court and jury what he said to you.

A: As we were leaving Las Vegas, before we were out of the city limits—Sheriff Robinson, Hickock and Mr. Church were in the lead car. Myself, Perry, and Mr. Duntz were following, and Perry could see in the car ahead and Hickock was talking, and Perry said to us, he says, 'Isn't he a tough guy?', meaning Hickock. He says, 'Look at him talk.' He said, 'Hickock had told me that if we were ever caught that we weren't going to say a word but there he is, just talking his head off.' He then asked me what Hickock said in regard to the killing of the Clutter family, who killed them. I told Perry that Hickock says that he killed all of the family. Perry told me that wasn't correct, but he said 'I killed two of them and Hickock killed two of them.'"

I drew several safe inferences from this testimony of law officers speaking under oath. First, contrary to Capote's account, Perry had begun to crack back in the Las Vegas Police Station. His remarks about Kenyon Clutter's radio clearly implicated him in the crime. Second, contrary to Capote's account, Dewey, Duntz, and Smith were not in the lead car; Smith would have seen nothing, except for a streak of desert highway had he turned around to look out the rear window at that moment. Third, contrary to Capote's account, Sherriff Robinson was in the lead car (Capote has Robinson on neither the trip to Las Vegas nor the return to Las Vegas nor the return to Garden City; maybe he did not sign the release—more about that later). Indeed, it was Robinson's car in the lead; the Garden City *Telegram*'s account of the trip chronicled a small crisis when Robinson's car suffered a burned-out wheel bearing in Lamar, Colorado, and Hickock had to be transferred twice to get him to Garden City. Fourth, contrary to Capote's account, it was not the "Nigger" incident that precipitated the sudden confession from Smith. Rather, it was simply Smith's observation of Hickock's loquaciousness in the lead car.

At this point I began to wonder about the disgusting "Nigger" incident. Had Dewey simply forgotten that by relating this story he had forced Smith to gasp and confess? The answer came later, in Duntz's testimony about the same events (pp. 276 to 282 in the transcript.). After establishing that he, Duntz, had first become acquainted with Smith in the "forepart of March, 1956" (a coincidence unmentioned in ICB), Duntz went on to mention the first time Smith had implicated himself in the Clutter case. The direct examination is by a man who was badly mischaracterized by Capote (more about that later): County Attorney Duane West.

"A: That was also at Police Headquarters and we were just making arrangements to leave and agent Nye was making preparations to go to look for a radio that we had information that had been taken. Perry was asked by Mr. Dewey if he cared to tell us where that was.

Q: Did he do so?

A: Yes, he did.

Q: What did he tell you at that time?

A. As I recall, he stated that it was in Mexico City to the same person who bought Richard Hickock's car.

Q: Mr. Duntz, what further conversation did you have with the defendant, if any?

A: Very little. I can't recall any there at Police Headquarters after that.

Q: Did you have any conversation with the defendant after you left Las Vegas?

A: It was soon after we had left Las Vegas en route to Kansas.

Q: Would you tell the jury just exactly what happened, as you recall it?

A. Perry Smith asked—do you mind if I clarify myself how we were riding?

Q: Go ahead.

A: I was riding in the car with Mr. Dewey and Perry Smith. They were riding in the front seat. I was in the back seat. The conversation was had between Perry Smith and Mr. Dewey. Perry asked Mr. Dewey if he could tell him what Dick had said about the murder and Mr. Dewey answered: 'Yes, Dick said that you killed all of them and Perry said 'That isn't right.' He said, 'He killed two and I killed two.'

Q: Was there any further conversation at that time, Mr. Duntz?

A: Well, at that time I told Perry of a conversation that I had had with Richard Hickock at Las Vegas, and that was Richard had told me soon after he had signed the statement that if I would tell Perry about a killing that Perry had told him about, and that pertained to an incident that was supposed to have happened previous to the time that Perry got in trouble—pardon me, in 1955, and Richard Hitchcock told me that if I would tell Perry Smith that Perry had told him that previous to that time he had killed a Nigger by clubbing him to death, then Perry would know that he, Richard Hickock, had been talking to us and giving us a statement.'"

Again, several safe inferences were drawn from this testimony. First, it corroborates Dewey's statement—establishing that Smith had begun to crack in the Las Vegas Police Station, establishing also that it was Dewey's answer to a question from Smith that preceded the confession. Second, contrary to Capote's account, the "Nigger" incident was related by the agents to Smith after he had admitted two of the slayings. Third, contrary to Capote's account, it was Duntz, not Dewey, who repeated the fictitious story to Smith.

We now have the word, given under oath, of two of the three principals to the climax of the novel. We can safely assume that this pair of professionals did not perjure themselves: can we be so sure of what Perry Smith may have told Capote? And if Capote favors Smith's version over the one given by Dewey and Duntz, is he not discrediting Dewey as a source? How then should we evaluate the remaining portions of the book in which we see events through Dewey's eyes?

So much for the manner of the confessions. What of the contents? During the trial, Dewey was forced to testify as to the substance of Smith's confession because the content was never signed by the defendant. Newspaper reports of Dewey's testimony at the trial (in the Garden City *Telegram* and the Hutchinson *News*, the latter gave the case the most extensive coverage in Kansas) do not square with Capote's version of the contents of the confession. Nevertheless, one might raise the possibility that Capote—by means of his relative intimacy with the principals—had been able to do a better job of reporting than these Kansas newspaper reporters who had to get their stories in the courtroom and hurriedly write them for publishing deadlines.

Here is Capote's account of Perry Smith's confession to the murder of Mr. Clutter, the first victim:

"Wait, I'm not telling it the way it was.' Perry scowls. He rubs his legs; the handcuffs rattle. 'After, see, after we'd taped them, Dick and I went off in a corner. To talk about it. Remember now, there were hard feelings between us. Just then it made my stomach turn to think I'd ever admired him, lapping up all that brag. I said, 'Well, Dick. Any qualms? He didn't answer me. I said 'Leave them alive and this won't be any small rap. Ten years the very least.' He still didn't say anything. He was holding the knife.

I asked him for it, and he gave it to me, and I said 'All right, Dick. Here goes.' But I didn't mean it. I meant to call his bluff, make him argue me out of it, make him admit he was a phony and a coward. See, it was something between me and Dick. I knelt down beside Mr. Clutter, and the pain of kneeling—I thought of that goddam dollar. Silver dollar. The shame. Disgust. And they'd told me never to come back to Kansas. But I didn't realize what I'd done till I heard the sound. Like somebody drowning. Screaming under water. I handed the knife to Dick. I said "Finish him. You'll feel better.' Dick tried—or pretended to. But the man had the strength of ten men—he was half out of his ropes, his hands were free. Dick panicked. Dick wanted to get the hell out of there. But I wouldn't let him go. The man would have died anyway. I know that, but I couldn't leave him like he was. I told Dick to hold the flashlight, focus it. Then I aimed the gun. The room exploded. Went blue. Just blazed up. Jesus, I'll never understand why they didn't hear the noise twenty miles around."

As a comparison, Dewey's testimony in the trial was as follow:

"So they debated who was going to do what and who was going to start it, and finally Smith said, 'Well,' he says, 'I'll do it,' so he said Hickock had the shotgun and the flashlight at this time and that he, Smith, had the knife and he said he put the knife in his hand with the blade up along his arm so Mr. Clutter couldn't see it and he walked over to where Mr. Clutter was laying on his mattress cover and he told him that he was going to tighten the cords on his hand, and he said he made a pretense to do that and then he cut Mr. Clutter's throat. Smith said that after doing that he got up and Hickock said 'Give me the knife' and he said that about that time they heard a gurgling sound coming from Mr. Clutter and Smith said that Hickock walked over to where Mr. Clutter was just as Smith was walking off this cardboard box, and he said he turned just for a second then Dick plunged this—Hickock plunged the knife into Mr. Clutter's throat, either once or twice. He said he couldn't tell which, but he heard the slap of the knife go in, and he said that he thought it went in full length because he heard a sound that went something –he described to me, something like this (indicating). He said after Hickock stepped away from Mr. Clutter that Mr. Clutter jerked one arm loose, his left arm, I believe, and he put into his throat to stop the bleeding and he said, 'Let's get the hell out of here,' and Smith said that he could see that Mr. Clutter was suffering and told Hickock that that was a hell of a way to leave a guy, because he felt he was going to die anyway, so Smith said he said to Hickock, 'Shall I shoot him?' and Hickock said, 'Yes, go ahead,' so Smith said that he shot Mr. Clutter in the head while Hickock held the flashlight. . . ."

These two versions differ in many little details, but the most serious discrepancy is the mental state of Perry Smith at the moment he begins the first murder. Capote has Smith say, "But I didn't mean it." And "But I didn't realize what I had done till

I heard the sound." (In the Plimpton interview, Capote referred to Smith's mental state at that moment as a "brain explosion.") Dewey, on the other hand, has Smith committing the murder with *full consciousness and intent.* On Dewey's word, the act was premeditated to the degree that Smith announced his intention, took pains to conceal the knife from the victim and deceived Mr. Clutter into thinking that he was just going to tighten his bonds. He made that pretense—and then cut his throat. The two versions clearly suggest different mental states.

In the article I anticipated three possible explanations that Capote might offer for these discrepancies: first, that the oral confession given during the automobile trip from Las Vegas was different from the statement Smith made upon arriving in Garden City (it was about the latter that Dewey was testifying); second, that Smith later told Capote details that he did not reveal while confessing to Dewey; and third, that Smith's later recollections of the confession (as told to Capote) were more accurate than Dewey's recollections (as told to the court).

We can dismiss the first explanation, that the confession in the car was different from the one dictated in the Sherriff's private office in Garden City. Capote describes, on p. 255, the second confession by saying it "recounted admissions already made to Alvin Dewey and Clarence Duntz." Furthermore, there is no indication in either the book or the transcript that the two confessions differed in any way.

The second possible explanation, that Smith told Capote details he had not revealed to Dewey, is undoubtedly true; Capote claims to have had more than 200 interviews with the killers. But to include those remarks is not to report the confession as it took place with law enforcement officers. And I doubt, for reasons to be discussed later, that Smith could have truthfully given such radically different versions of the confession. (Wendell Meier, former Undersheriff of Finney County, told me that he had visited Smith at Lansing; that Smith told him that there would be inaccuracies in the book; when Mr. Meier asked him what these would be, Smith would only say—read it and see for yourself.)

The third possible explanation, that Smith's later recollections of the confession as told to Capote were more accurate than Dewey's testimony, is not difficult to refute. Duntz's testimony in the transcript corroborates Dewey's testimony in every way. More conclusive is the fact that Dewey gave an extremely accurate account of the contents of the confession. I know because I have examined it. As I said in the *Esquire* article, "it is now in the possession of former County Attorney West." It may still be there. He let me read it while interviewing him. I believe he said that it was in his possession because Smith would not sign his copy because he later changed his confession to take the blame for all four killings to give solace to members of Hickock's family. Here is what I read and copied in West's office:

". . . I think we was debating who was going to do what and who was going to start it, so I told him, 'Well,' I says, I'll do it, so I walked over to Mr. Clutter and he couldn't hear us talk from where we was over at the door. We was kind of talking in a whisper. I walked over to Mr. Clutter and Dick come over close. He had the flashlight and had the shotgun in his hand and I would say he was standing, oh, about at Mr. Clutter's head and I told him I was going to tie his hands a little tighter and he was laying on his right side and he was taped then. He didn't say anything or he didn't mumble and, well, as I made a pretense to tie his hands again I cut Mr. Clutter's throat. That's when I cut Mr. Clutter's throat, and he started to struggle and I got up right away and Dick says, 'Give me that knife.' I could see he was nervous and that's when the gurgling sound of Mr. Clutter was noticed . . .'"

This was the most important paragraph in my article, "In Cold Fact." When Capote bought a copy of the magazine at the newsstand, as Editor Dobell wanted, he must have realized that the truth was out when he read the *real* confession. Here we have Perry Smith's own words, taken down verbatim and signed by a certified court stenographer, Lillian C. Valenzuela. There is not the slightest hint or implication of either "brain explosion," "mental eclipse," or "schizophrenic eclipse" at the crucial moment. The comments in quotation marks are ways Capote expressed to describe Perry's mental state in interviews with reviewers and journalists. This is the climax of "In Cold Fact." Capote clearly identified with Perry Smith and tried to turn him into *le poete maudit*, the accursed poet. I have not counted the number of grammatical errors in that one paragraph of discourse, but a poet Perry was not.

Now we shall turn to another significant part of the book—the conclusion. In the final chapter of *In Cold* Blood we see the execution of the killers. Hickock was hanged first. Smith was brought into the warehouse and asked if he wished to make a statement. Those last words, as quoted by Capote are: "'I think," he said, "it's a helluva thing to take a life in this manner. I don't believe in capital punishment, morally or legally. Maybe I had something to contribute, something.' His assurance faltered; shyness blurred his voice, lowered it to a just audible level. 'It would be meaningless to apologize for what I did. Even inappropriate. But I do. I apologize.'"

Bill Brown, Editor of the Garden City *Telegram,* represented the Kansas newspapers as a witness of the execution. He stood four feet away from Smith when Smith's last words were spoken (Capote was unable to watch; he walked away, out of earshot.) Brown took notes. He immediately compared his notes with those of wire-service representatives standing on either side of him—they were identical. Here are Smith's words as recorded and reported by Brown in the *Telegram* of April 14, 1965:

"Asked if he had anything to say before mounting the gallows, Smith stated 'Yes, I would like to say a word or two. I think it is a hell of a thing that a life has to be taken in this manner. I say this especially because there's a great deal I could have offered society. I certainly think capital punishment is legally and morally wrong.

Any apology for what I have done would be meaningless at this time. I don't have any animosities toward anyone involved in this matter. I think that is all.'"

In 1966 I wrote "Brown is today convinced that Smith did not apologize." I wrote Tony Jewell of Garden City's radio station KIUL; he was the first radio newscaster to be invited to witness an execution in Kansas. Immediately after the execution, Jewell and Brown telephoned their reports to the radio station in Garden City; the remarks were recorded for later broadcast. I have a tape recording of that broadcast; again, there was not an apology from Smith. Furthermore, there is no indication of an apology in the Associated Press story that was filed that day."

"In Cold Fact" also contained these comments:

"Finally, in a telephone conversation with Alvin A. Dewey on February 5, I asked him how Capote had obtained Smith's words (in the book it is through Dewey's eyes and ears that we see and hear these events.) Mr. Dewey did not know. 'Perhaps he overheard me talking about it later,' he suggested. Had Perry apologized? Mr. Dewey could not recall Perry's exact words, but thought they were 'something along that line.' What is certain is that Capote did not hear Perry's words at first hand. Dewey, the narrator of the event in the book, is now unsure how Capote got the information. Capote's reconstruction, then, conflicts with the report by two newsmen who made their notes on the spot—not sometime later, which is the method of recording Capote tells us he used. The best evidence supports the conclusion that Perry Smith did not apologize."

I also wanted to answer a question raised by Rebecca West in her review of *In Cold Blood* in *Harper's*: "Hickock was hanged for a murder which he had not committed, when he should have been sentenced to a term of imprisonment as an accessory, but this was not his own fault. The truth could only be established if both he and Perry chose to give evidence, but this, for a reason Mr. Capote does not explain, they did not do."

Who would know?

The files of the Garden City *Telegram* and Hutchinson *News* pointed me to the best source. They showed that former County Attorney Duane West played the most significant role in the case after the murders were discovered. He was on the scene of the crime the day the bodies were discovered; he was involved in the investigation from beginning to end; he held daily press conferences; he prepared the brief and the trial outline for the case; he asked the Finney County Commissioners for permission to hire an assistant—Logan Green; he gave the opening remarks for the prosecution;

he represented the County and State in the appeal before the Supreme Court of Kansas. As I read the newspaper accounts it was as if I was reading another nonfiction account of the trial.

In the article as published by *Esquire* I wrote parenthetically: "(In the book, however, West is made to appear somewhat lower in rank than a law clerk)." But then I thought, *my article will restore him to his proper status as the hero of the case.* After "In Cold Fact" came out I was disappointed that it seemed not to produce that effect.

When I raised Rebecca West's question, West told me it made no difference whether Hickock killed any or all of the Clutters. Under the Felony Murder Rule, which applies in Kansas and many other states, any party to a felony in which a life is taken can be prosecuted for murder. "If you and I conspired to rob a store," West explained, "and I killed someone while robbing it—you could be tried for murder." He also told me he had decided to try Smith and Hickock together when it became known they might request separate trials. West then moved to have their names added to the list of witnesses (which he could not do if they were to be tried together.) "Our feeling was that Perry would testify against Dick. He was willing to take the blame for all four killings to make it easier for Hickock's mother, but he was not willing to take the blame for the plan."

West told me on two occasions that he believed Smith's confession to be true—that Hickock killed the two Clutter women. Another man intimate with the case from the beginning to the end, Bill Brown, agrees that Hickock did two of the killings. And so, apparently did Alvin A. Dewey. When asked, during the trial, why he would not allow Smith to change his confession (to take the blame for all four murders), Dewey explained that Smith and Hickock had been able to shout back and forth from their respective cells and negotiate the changes. They knew that, regardless of the details of the confessions, they would both "hang." Smith was willing to make the changes to spare Hickock's family that much pain. The clear implication of the testimony is that Dewey did not believe Smith. The most we can say for Capote on this point is that it was poor reporting to lead such a careful reader as Rebecca West to the confident conclusion that Smith had committed all the Clutter murders while the principals were less than unanimous.

Why did he make the changes?

While writing "In Cold Fact," I had to be careful not to accuse Capote of lying. That is why I wrote this short paragraph: "Before offering my hypotheses for these discrepancies, let me state that Capote's awareness of the errors is not at stake. It is conceivable that they were completely unintentional. As Capote told Jane Howard of *Life*, within three weeks of each interview he retreated to his motel, wrote up his notes and filed them. "'Funnily enough,' he said, 'I seldom had to look at my notes after that: I had it all in my head." The transformation of facts may well have resulted from his failure to consult his notes more closely.

Capote himself has given us a broad, general hypothesis to explain the discrepancies. A non-fiction novel is more difficult than a conventional novel, he said to *Life*, because "you have to get away from your own particular vision of the world." But apparently Capote did not succeed in doing so; he presumably still needed that very conventional element of the novel as he knew it—a dramatic climax, a moment of truth. The subtle but significant distorting of the facts to fit a preconception of the novelistic, which turned an extraordinarily unexciting confession into a theatrical catharsis.

The transformation of the contents of the confession demands a more extended explanation. A close inspection of the characterization of Perry Smith is necessary. Capote was drawn to him more than to Hickock. It is Perry Smith—not the victims, not the investigators, not the lawyers, not even the pair of killers—who dominates this book. Why the attraction? When Smith stood up, wrote Capote, "he was no taller than a twelve-year old child." The Avedon photographs of the two standing together reveal that Capote, if anything, is a "slippery spray" of hair shorter than Smith. Furthermore, Smith had a miserable childhood. Harper Lee, who had known Capote long and well, told *Newsweek*, "I think every time Truman looked at Perry he saw his own childhood."

But there the similarities –which may have attracted Capote to Smith—would appear to end. Smith, after all, lived in a world of violence. A measure of the emotional gap between them is that Perry invented a tale in which he had beaten a Negro to death. It was a boast, calculated to increase the esteem in which his friend Dick held him. Capote, on the other hand, told Haskel Frankel of the *Saturday Review*: "I am not interested in crime per se: I hate violence."

It is my hypothesis that in his vision of the world, Capote found it difficult if not impossible to understand how a man could kill, could kill without feeling. He could understand, however, that an outcast and accursed poet might kill while under a mental eclipse, while deep inside a schizophrenic darkness—a "brain explosion" if you will—and thus avenge the wrongs "they" had done him. Once out of the mental eclipse, necessarily, he would be "embraced by shame." And hesitantly tender his apologies.

And so the facts were transformed. Perry Smith, who could hardly get a grammatical sentence out of his mouth while dictating his confession, becomes *le poete maudit* and corrects the grammar in newspaper articles about him. To judge from the confession, Perry Smith was an obscene, semi-literate and cold-blooded killer. But as Yuric correctly guessed in the *Nation*, we cannot rest with the Perry Smiths as they are: "Before we kill them we make sure they negate themselves by turning into literate, psychopathic heroes."

By having Smith say, "I didn't know what I was doing," Capote projected his own vision of the world on to Smith at that moment. In doing so he created a hybrid of Capote-Smith predispositions and the real Smith becomes even less understandable. Should we believe he suffered a "brain explosion" when he poised the rock to open the head of the Omaha salesman? And again when he wished out loud that he could have killed his sister along with the Clutters? And when he planned with Hickock two other murders which Capote told Plimpton he chose to omit from the book? Capote appears to have fallen into the trap of believing that misguided operational definition of insanity one frequently hears: "Anyone who can kill has to be insane."

Perry's values toward human life derived from a world in which men expect to kill and be killed. He explained these values quite succinctly (and demonstrated just how much shame he felt) to his friend, Donald Cullivan on page 291. Perry insisted that he was not sorry for what he had done; he was only sorry that he could not walk out of the cell with his visitor. Cullivan, like Capote, could scarcely believe that Perry was so devoid of conscience and compassion.

Perry said "Why? Soldiers don't lose much sleep. They murder, and get medals for doing it. The good people of Kansas want to murder me—and some hangman will be glad to get the work. It's easy to kill—a lot easier than passing a bad check."

For this set of values, Capote substituted his own. By so doing, the murder of the Clutters became more understandable to Capote and his readers. From there it was just a short step to impart to Perry qualities of inner sensitivity, poetry and a final posture of contrition. The killer now evokes considerable sympathy. He cries. He asks to have his hand held. He says, "I'm embraced by shame." He apologizes. But none of this is convincing to me. The remorse, the fine phrases and last-word apology came from the lips of the same man who told his friend Cullivan he was not sorry, the same man who would not play the hypocrite with Cullivan or his friend Willie-Jay.

In describing Perry, Capote wrote: "His own face enthralled him. Each angle of it induced a different impression. It was a changeling's face." In *Newsweek* Capote described himself: "If you looked at my face from both sides you'd see they were completely different. It's sort of a changeling's face." And when Jane Howard of *Life* asked him whether or not he liked Perry and Dick, he said, "That's like saying, "Do you like yourself?" Capote's characterization of Smith clearly tells us more about the former than the latter. Capote set out to write an objective book, but rather than annihilate his own personality, he has produced a highly subjective work, projecting himself into the dominant personality of the novel.

How can we explain Capote's unwillingness to deal completely with the question of Hickock's involvement in the killings? It makes for a more simplified narrative in an already complex book to let readers assume there was unanimity among the principals on the point. But, in addition, Capote's conception of the novel places high value on irony; he wants to believe the murders were emotional, spontaneous acts. (After examining the evidence, the title becomes a double irony.) Other examples of this fondness for this technique are the ironic twists at the end of so many chapters. And how much more ironic to present the true, the only, killer in the case as the more appealing of the two.

Capote has, in short, achieved a work of art. He has told exceedingly well a tale of high terror in his own way. But despite the brilliance of his self-publicizing efforts, he has made both a tactical and moral mistake that will hurt him in the short run. By insisting that "every word" of his work is true has made himself vulnerable to those readers who are prepared to examine such a sweeping claim. In the long run, however, Capote's presumption will be forgotten. The living people who were involved in the case will no longer testify to another version of the story. The documents will have been pushed to the back of the files by other, more urgent, matters and crime. Future literary historians and scholars will undoubtedly place Capote's discrepancies of fact as well as his pretensions and rationalizations in perspective, and they will join with the present and future public in enjoying the work for its own sake. "Time . . . " as Auden wrote, "worships language and forgives Everybody by whom it lives . . . ."

Chapter Six
Fifteen Minutes of Fame

The final paragraph of the previous chapter was also the final paragraph of "In Cold Fact." Strange as it may sound, it was *not* written by the author, me, rather it was by *Esquire*'s legal staff, so as not to incite a legal action by Truman Capote's lawyers. I did not like it then and do not like it any better today. I had planned to begin this chapter with my own paragraph but in preparing this book I discovered that *Esquire*'s lawyers had also deleted the four important paragraphs leading up to the final one. So now I begin anew with the words leading up to and including my concluding paragraph. I had begun my complaint that the main character and the most heroic figure in the Clutter case was made by Capote to appear a minor figure, a Kansas country rube whose shoes squeaked when he took a step in the courtroom. The next five paragraphs were, and still are, in my final, edited and approved manuscript, but they did not appear in the article. This is the first time they have ever been in print. I will not put quote marks at the beginning or end so that the reader can see how it should have looked in *Esquire*. Here are *my* final paragraphs:

A much simpler explanation for the inaccurate depiction of the County Attorney's role in the case may be given. I confronted West with the question as to why he had been written out of the book. His reply was "Probably because I didn't sign the release." The "release" was described by the Kansas City *Star* (January 27) as follows:

"On the surface, the release gave Capote the right to use the names in a movie, but some lawyers who studied the case say the ones they saw were much broader, giving the author the right to 'tell the story as he saw fit.'"

West's reason for declining to sign the release, however, was that he felt it pre-empted his right ever to write anything about the case. "I may want to write something on it someday," he said.

Except for this final, dramatic reason, the best explanation for the distortions of fact throughout *In Cold Blood* is that Capote could not get away from his own personality and values, his own vision of the world, his own particular conception of the novel. What has he gained? Final curtains for some of his internal short dramas.

A theatrical climax. A heroic, poetic villain—a villain capable of evoking considerable sympathy. Should we have expected anything different from Capote? His good friend, Harper Lee, told *Newsweek:* "He knows what he wants and he keeps himself straight. And if it's not the way he likes it, he'll arrange it so it is."

But what has he lost? Persuasiveness. A chance to demonstrate that reality is not fiction; that events in the real world often have diffused, faltering climaxes—even cardboard characters. He has lost the chance to present the truth so that each reader could find his own pattern, conclusion, and diagnosis. He has lost the chance to demonstrate the unity of truth. He has lost the chance to provide the answer to *why*? And the reader, also, has lost something: the faith that he, with diligence, might infer an even greater truth from reliable data.

Note the fourth from last word in what I wrote: "Truth." Today I am proud that I used the word "truth" in that paragraph, but I also wish I had used the word "she" as well as the masculine term. But the reader must wonder why *Esquire*'s editors and lawyers cut those five paragraphs and substituted that new one for *their* fifth and final paragraph. As mentioned above, their lawyers feared a suit because they feared my words accused Capote of "mendacity." But, why the others? Duane West was the hero of the case. He was the Finney County Attorney who was on the case immediately and successfully prosecuted the case. Capote reduced his role to the least possible extent. Why?

Because of the *release* he would not sign. I had not heard of the release until he, West, mentioned it during one of our two interviews. The release allowed Capote to put any words into the mouth of a person who had signed it. How does that square with the claim that every word they spoke as presented *in ICB* was true? That is the dark secret of *In Cold Blood*, but *Esquire*'s lawyers made it a legal secret by editing these paragraphs out of "In Cold Fact." Today in 2021 I am much more disturbed that they deleted those words than my concluding paragraph. Why? Because Duane West had clearly emerged in the role of the hero of the story. I wanted him to be the hero of my nonfiction version of the Clutter case. He did not sign the release because he might one day tell his story: the truth. And he told the truth to me. Duane West, so far as I know, is still alive, in his nineties. I want him to see these words in print and know that the rest of the readers now know who was and still is, and always will be the hero of the Clutter Case: Duane West.

"Antebellum Antimacassar"

My phone did ring after "In Cold Fact" was published. I had calls from newspapers around the country. The New York *Times* mentioned my article briefly. So did the Kansas City *Star*. A letter to the Editor of mine about *In Cold Blood* and "In Cold Fact" was much later published in *The New Yorker*. After an article about "In Cold Fact" appeared in the Detroit *Free Press*, I ran into the reporter who wrote it at a baseball game at Tiger Stadium; he had a frown on his face as he pressed me about my *motives*. Motives. I would hear much more about those things. Then I was invited to spend an hour or so with a talk show host on Detroit's most popular radio station at the time, WJR as I recall. I do not remember the name of the program's host, but he was highly popular, cordial, inquisitive, and generous with praise, saying that I was so young that he had a lot to look forward to from me in the future.

The producer of the program took me by the arm at the end of my interview and moved me over to another chair away from the action, until he could show me the door at the next commercial break. He started to walk away but turned back and asked,

"Would you be willing to debate Truman Capote on the air?"

"Yes, I would be willing and have not used all of my material."

"He is a friend of mine and so I will ask him if he is interested in debating you. I came to know him through a mutual friend."

I nodded.

"He is gayer than an antebellum antimacassar, just to let you know in advance."

I nodded again and got up to go home and check on that phrase. *Antebellum* I knew means before the war and often refers to the U.S. Civil War. That made sense because literary critics referred to Capote's prose as Southern Gothic. *Antimacassar* I had to look up in that Shorter *OED*: "A covering thrown over sofas, chairs, etc., to protect them from grease in the hair, etc., or as an ornament." The producer did not smile when he said it, nor did I in response. But when I told the story to others they often laughed and asked for the definition of antimacassar. I was only slightly disappointed not to hear from the producer about another debate.

I had moved up to a studio apartment in Lafayette Park with a great view of downtown Detroit and a piece of Canada that juts into our land. On my way to the outdoor swimming pool, I overheard a small group of people talking about the Detroit man who had written an article about *In Cold Blood*. I wanted to jump into the discussion, but I decided to jump into the water instead. I heard congratulations, of course, from relatives and friends. I visited my former wife and our kids in Rapid City later that summer. Their mother had a male friend, a local businessman she said, who read "In Cold Fact."

"And?"

"He says you are a perfectionist."

Later I remembered Kenneth Burke's "Definition of Man" which I used to teach to my classes after changing it to Human; one of the defining characteristics is "Rotten with perfection."

A Visit to New York

My closest colleague at Wayne State became my closest friend in Detroit: Edward J. Pappas. He introduced me to a friend of his who wanted to put us to use as consultants teaching communication to business managers. I could use the money, to help with alimony and child support, so I accompanied the two of them on a trip to New York City. We had a couple of business meetings, but they gave me enough time to schedule a meeting at *Esquire*. A staff member showed me into the office of Editor Byron Dobell. He seemed pleased to meet me and asked me where I lived.

"Detroit," I answered, and later wondered if he had read "In Cold Fact" because the first paragraph of the article mentioned that I drove from Detroit to Garden City and bak. He seemed surprised.

"Well, it will be good to have someone out there."

We stood, shook hands, and as I started to leave his office, he suggested that I make an appointment with the Research Editor of the magazine. I got in to see her, a pleasant young woman whose name I have sadly forgotten. She reminded me that after I mailed in the manuscript of "In Cold Fact," she called to ask me to mail her my documents: interview notes, names, and the phone number of every person I quoted in the article. I did so and forgot all about her. But now she showed me one whole section of her office that was a stockpile, boxes of files and other papers about "In Cold Fact." Everyone she called said "Yes, that is what I told Mr. Tompkins." One hundred percent: Rotten with perfection. She even showed me the notes taken during her phone call to the Supreme Court of the State of Kansas in Topeka.

Replication of a Replication!

"Yes," she said, "they confirmed that you had visited them, read the transcript of the trial and had even paid for copies they made of some pages." I was dumbfounded. She supplied me with the information providing me with a great insight. When the time did come for me to achieve a full realization, I was able to put it into words: I had conducted a *replication* of Truman Capote's literary experiment and found that the book failed to meet the test. Capote was like the former graduate student in Chemistry at Purdue whose dissertation failed in a replication attempt of it.

But then there was a *second* replication, one in which my method of research was itself replicated in part and it succeeded, a *successful replication*. It was more interesting to me and others, I expect, than the Chemistry experiment for a couple of reasons. One, a double replication, putting together a failed replication and a successful replication to determine the truth. Two, we had moved out of the scientific laboratory and into the study of literature, human communication, "social" science, and journalism. I was excited. Later I realized that the villainous lawyer-editors had failed to replicate perfectly the *expression* of my findings, by cutting five paragraphs and offering a one-paragraph substitution for them. Yes, it is a complicated process, but again we were dealing with the humanities and social sciences, not the simpler, more easily achieved rigor of the lab experiment.

Esquire sent me a check for $600 and I made a black and white copy of it I still have. Over the years "In Cold Fact" has been reprinted in anthologies of literary criticism, e. g. *Contemporary Literary Criticism. Esquire* held the rights to the essay and was good about sending me the fees assessed for granting permission to reprint it. An Editor at the *Quarterly Journal of Speech*, Professor David Berg, asked me for an essay that we called "The Rhetorical Criticism of Non-Oratorical Works," which is said to have influenced many people in the field of communication to move beyond the study of oral rhetoric and tackle literature, and other human artifices in their rhetorical studies and publications.

A Lesson in the Meaning of Life

Colleagues at Wayne State University congratulated me on the work. At least most of them. Word got back to me that the Chair of the Speech Communication Department had told others that if an article by one of his professors could be read in a barber shop, it would not be worth reading. Others were supportive and I met with some of them from other departments at Verne's, a kind of diner with a bar located a block or two off campus. We began to meet in the late afternoon and then began to assign readings for the next meeting. We selected a translation of *The Myth of Sisyphus* by Albert Camus. It was published in 1942 by the Existentialist author who received a Nobel Prize for Literature in 1957. The book deals with a topic of study in many academic disciplines. A short book, I read it in one sitting with great interest. I could hardly wait to get to the meeting at about 4:00 p.m.

Camus tells the myth in a new way. Yes, Sisyphus is condemned to hell for eternity, pushing a boulder up an incline. Once he gets it to the top he steps aside and allows it to slide or roll to the bottom of the decline. Do not feel sorry for him, teaches Camus, for he is pleased, comforted to know that life is *absurd*. We reveled in our commentaries about this absurdity. But then I realized that I was late for a date with Miss Mack, a lovely lady in one of the same Lafayette Towers in which I now dwelled. I apologized for leaving my academic friends so hurriedly; I must have been speeding because I was pulled over on the way home by a police officer.

"Let me see your driver's license," he ordered.

I pulled it out and did not realize I had a problem until he told me:

"This license has expired. I am taking you in."

He arranged to have my car towed while taking me to jail in his car. As I was being "booked," as they say, I could hear the arresting officer say to others in the back room, with what I deemed to be a sense of pride,

"I brought in a professor tonight."

Cheers followed.

I was told I could make one phone call when the phone was available. I was then put in a long holding cell with maybe ten men, most of them Black. I was devastated. Then they said it was time for me to make a phone call. I called Miss Mack, apologized, and asked her to come to the station, and bring some cash to lend me for bail money. She said she would be able to do so.

As I waited for her to bail me out, I sat on the bench reflecting on the day of teaching, reading, and oh, yes, the wonderful discussion of Camus' Myth. I broke out laughing, loudly.

"What is so funny?" asked an angry Black man who stopped his pacing to ask the question.

"Life is absurd."

Without hesitation, he replied as he turned and began pacing again:

"No, man. Life is a mother-fucker."

I stopped laughing and contemplated what he said and what it meant to him. It also taught me a lesson about trying to produce or find theories that specify a philosophic truth with a *universal* meaning about human existence. In addition, the truth does not have the same meaning for all who perceive it. Think of the graduate student in Chemistry at Purdue, who faked the results and was caught. And the results of my replication could not have made Capote as happy as those friends I heard from after

"In Cold Fact" hit the newsstands and libraries.

Now that I reflect on it, Richard Hickok and Perry Smith might have agreed with my cellmate's existential pronouncement: Life *is* a motherfucker.

Who knew except Capote what he had gone through in his definition of existence? We do know the childhood was miserable for its lack of love. In addition, he must have been bullied and shamed because of his small size and effeminate way of acting. He could identify with Perry Smith and perhaps even felt affection for him. That is why I came to believe that *In Cold Blood* the title was *not* about the Clutter murders. Despite what we know by having Perry's authentic confession, Capote wanted us to know and believe that Perry Smith did not know what he was doing when he cut Mr. Clutter's throat. He wanted us to believe it was the opposite of his title, *In Cold Blood*, with the ironic twist. As a reference to the Clutter killings the title should have been *In Hot Blood*. But how about the judge, prosecutor, and jurors who listened to all the evidence and agreed—in their cold- blooded procedures—to have two young men hang by the neck until they died. The title can be read as a rhetorical or persuasive attack on capital punishment.

I was against capital punishment all my few adult years until I read *In Cold Blood* and visited Garden City and Holcomb, Kansas in order to replicate Capote's methods of gathering data. While there I did save time to visit the Clutter house in Holcomb. I parked my car at a respectful distance from it and walked about, looking at and contemplating what had happened in it. From the book and newspaper files I had learned that the mother and daughter were tied up in their respective beds upstairs. The father and son were tied up in the basement. When Mr. Clutter struggled to get free, all four could hear the first shotgun blast. A pause, a break in time and then three Clutters could knowingly hear the second blast. The women could probably hear the killers walking up the stairs and then hear the third blast.

Then I thought of Mrs. Clutter. She must have lain there counting not sheep, not just shotgun blasts, but the deaths of her loved ones: Herbert, Kenyon, Nancy, and now: here they come for me. After hearing the death sentences of the three, she may have wanted that last blast to find her. No, I am sure that if someone could have asked her if life is absurd, she would have disagreed, and would be much closer in her belief to my cellmate than to Camus, even if with a different word choice. I walked slowly around the front of the house thinking of all four of them and I was at that sad moment satisfied with capital punishment for Hickock and Smith. And for Lowell Lee Andrews, cold-blooded killer of his parents and sister.

Capote's Response to In Cold Fact

Some of Capote's hostile reaction to "In Cold Fact" did get back to me indirectly. For example, when I learned his book would become a movie, I called Michael Curtis at the *Atlantic* to see if they would be interested in an article about possible changes in the screenplay, i.e., whether it would be modified because of my alternative set of facts.

"Yes," said Michael, "and I'll get to work on getting you the credentials to visit the studio in Hollywood and the location in Kansas on our behalf."

"Great."

The next word I got was that the *Atlantic* got a telegram from Hollywood saying that "Phil Tompkins is not welcome on either the set or the location of this film."

But then I was approached by the Michigan State Newspaper Association which was having a convention. A leader of the Association asked me about speaking to them about the factuality of the film, and whether the film makers had made any changes because of "In Cold Fact." The plan was to get a review copy of the film we could all watch together, the state's newspaper representatives and me. At the conclusion I would give an extemporaneous speech about facts and fantasy, then take questions from the audience. I thought it would be fun and a compliment for my method of finding and reporting the truth. The officers were pleased that I accepted and then came word from Hollywood that there would be no review copies made available to any newspaper in the State of Michigan, the whole state. We would have to pay to see it in a theater, presumably to avoid bad reviews before its general release.

Then there was a function at the University of Kansas about the book, to which Capote had been invited, but I had not. At a cocktail reception later, Truman discovered that Dr. Bill Conboy, Chair of the Department of Speech Communication and Theater, knew Phil Tompkins. He steered Bill into a corner and interrogated him at considerable length.

"What is Tompkins' motive?" This was the question Capote kept pressing Bill about. Bill told me about it before much time had passed since the event and it helped me conclude that Capote did not fully understand me and my motives. My hypothesis is that because he did not attend college, he apparently did not appreciate that faculty members are committed to an overarching value premise: finding, knowing, validating, and teaching the *truth,* even without a capital "T." It also dawned on me that Capote's deal with his interviewees, the "release," should have prevented me from discovering the truth. I am forever grateful to those interviewees such as Bill Brown, Editor of the Garden City *Telegram,* and especially Duane West, former Finney County Attorney;

both of whom were so committed to the truth they cooperated with me to produce "In Cold Fact," at least in its manuscript form and the printed form as corrected in this book.

Over the years I have been recognized for what people read in my published article, "In Cold Fact," including a student in Scotland who recently reached me via email so he could ask me to help him find a copy of my article. My friend and colleague at the University of Colorado at Denver, Dr. Omar Swartz, helped me find a way to send a photographic copy of the article to the writer in Scotland. Omar also set me up a few years ago with a Skype in a conference room near his office so that I could interact with a literature class at Princeton University reading *In Cold Blood.*

I shall now bring this chapter to a close by revealing my anger in discovering while writing this book that all the people in the world who read *In Cold Blood* and "In Cold Fact" do not know who the real hero of this horrible mass murder is and why. In addition to my anger, I am also experiencing a measure of satisfaction that with this book readers will now finally realize the story has a shining knight, Mr. Duane West. The Finney County Attorney who was on the Clutter case from the first day, who successfully prosecuted the cold-blooded killers, and who refused to sign the "release" which would have taken away his legal right to tell me the truth. And by acting out his commitment to the *truth* adds to his great honor.

Open Communication

Duane West's commitment to the truth was manifest in his practice of open communication with me during my two interviews with him, by telling me about the court case, showing me Perry's confession, and telling me about the transcript of the trial at the Supreme Court of Kansas in Topeka. I must also point out that part of my replication was possible because of open communication practiced by Bill Brown, Editor of the Garden City *Telegram*. He sat me down to read two newspaper files so that I would have a journalistic overview of the case. He was open with me about Perry Smith's confession, what was said and not said. Yes, the replication was possible because these men practiced open communication with the replicator.

Recall that the Research Editor at *Esquire* successfully replicated my work because I practiced open communication with her. Yes, I supplied her with the name and phone number of every person I quoted in the article. She was open with them, and my sources were open with her. Once again replication seems to work well only if conducted with open communication.

Chapter Seven
A Phone Call from the Heavens

After devoting so much of my time to "In Cold Fact" vs. *In Cold Blood* I could now afford to get back into the arts, reading more James Joyce, and American writers such as Hemingway, Steinbeck, and Fitzgerald. Once more I was a regular listener at the concerts of the Detroit Symphony Orchestra as well as playing my own growing LP Classical vinyl records; I also learned to enjoy the local culture, the artists at Motown Records. I even bought a new album called Sgt. Pepper's Lonely Hearts Club Band. Students and other friends recommended it and I was rather surprised by how much I enjoyed it. Many years later I would watch a documentary on PBS with an expert on classical music who developed the theme that some of the Beatles' songs employed important techniques of classical music.

But I had neglected the main concentration in my graduate work during the literary adventure: Organizational Communication. I got back to doing workshops for automobile manufacturing management groups and the United Auto Workers Union. And then it came.

The man on the phone said, with the slightest of German accent, that his name was Walter Wiesman (pronounced "Veesman"), and that he was calling from Huntsville, Alabama. He said his title was the Coordinator of Internal Communication at NASA's George C. Marshall Space Flight Center.

The name and accent of the caller, his job title, and organization got the full, rapt attention of Associate Professor Dr. Phillip K. Tompkins. This could be an opportunity. I needed to know why he was calling me. Wiesman did not make me wait long.

"I would like to offer you an appointment as a Summer Faculty Consultant to the Marshall Center." I felt the rush and after a pause I began to regain control, asking him to repeat what he said. He did, and then Wiesman explained that the consultancy program had been put in place to bring in experts in engineering and scientific disciplines. (I would be the first "soft scientist" to serve as Summer Faculty Consultant, as a fellow summer consultant put it to me later.) As I came to understand what this meant I felt the thrill of my short lifetime.

If I accepted, Wiesman continued, I would be responsible for helping him organize what would later be called by W. Charles Redding the *first* conference ever devoted only to papers delivered on Organizational Communication. We would invite people in government, business, and the academic world to the meetings to be held in Huntsville that summer. I would deliver the keynote address. I would evaluate Wiesman's program in Internal Communication and report it to the Marshall Center leaders. I would also guide a graduate student through his dissertation at the Marshall Center, a student from Purdue University named Gary Richetto. Finally, I would also do research requested by the Director of the Marshall Space Flight Center. For all of this I would be paid a salary at the rate of a GS-13 in the Civil Service system. I did not tell Mr. Wiesman I would have agreed to do it for nothing as community service at the national level and as research for publication.

I had followed rocketry in the news as a boy from World War II up to the then present. That made it possible and desirable to ask,

"Isn't that where Dr. Wernher von Braun is heading up the research on the Moon Rocket?"

"Yes," Wiesman answered, "He is Director of the Marshall Space Flight Center and, yes, we are doing the Research and Development for the Saturn Rocket to be used in the Apollo Project." He did not need to add that von Braun had developed the first rocket to be used in warfare, the V-2. That first rocket rained on the Netherlands and Great Britain.

Remembering I had kept the next summer free of commitments so that I could do some research and writing gave me the freedom to accept the offer on the spot! Or at that moment! Mr. Wiesman said he would find an apartment for me near the Space Center in Huntsville. He said he would also arrange for me to have an office near his. Finally, he said he would send me materials so that I could begin my application for a high security clearance, reminding me I would be entering the serious Space Race between the U.S.S.R. and the U.S.A. during the Cold War. The Federal Bureau of Investigation would send me a questionnaire in which I had to indicate all interactions over a long period of time, as I recall. It was laborious. I heard from a few people who were curious as to why the FBI questioned them carefully about me.

Then I recalled that it was on May 21, 1961, that President John F. Kennedy, one of my favorites in that job, had promised that the U.S. would land a man on the Moon within the decade of the 1960s. Here we were with only about three years in which to accomplish the goal. Could my work help keep the promise? I was thrilled and enjoyed telling others about my appointment.

While most people thought of it as a personal triumph for Phil Tompkins, I knew that it was much more than that. It would give a form of accreditation, or *validation*, to our new field of Organizational Communication. It would be a success for Purdue

University for having given birth to the new program. It would also be a vindication for W. Charles Redding, the Purdue Professor of Speech who had initiated the study of Organizational Communication. *Validation* of our new field, the word and its meaning, kept coming to mind, at both the personal and program levels. Oh, and this could help the educational revolution, the change from a field of Speech to one of Communication.

I had another concern that bothered me: I was greatly concerned about race relations in the Deep South, but I did not hesitate to accept the offer. I could not have anticipated that race relations in Huntsville, Alabama would prove to be better than I expected. Dr. von Braun did all he could to improve them while race riots broke out all over Detroit, Michigan; I would be having trouble making sense out of them from articles in the local Huntsville *Times* that summer.

I drove from Detroit to Huntsville, getting there late at night in the early summer of 1967. I checked into a rather sleezy motel on the Huntsville strip. In the morning of the next day, I called Walter Wiesman; he gave me directions to meet him at the apartment he had taken in my name. He was younger than I thought he would be, a handsome man with good interpersonal communication skills and a slight, charming accent. He gave me directions to the Space Center and a temporary entry card until I could get my security badge. Again, I said to myself, *this is the Cold War*, after all, and the security was as tight as at a military base, or so I was told. They want to make sure I am not a Commie who will reveal secrets to the USSR. The temporary card got me through the checkpoint the next morning.

On my first day on the job, I met the people in Walt's office with what in retrospect had a rather sexist word in the title: "Manpower." It slightly suggested participation in the Cold War. I was shown to my desk: on it was a phone and a beautiful piece of wood with my name painted in Gothic letters and holes in the top hold pencils and pens: *High Quality Control*, I said to myself. Then began my awesome orientation program.

Orientation to the Marshall Center

For the first part of my orientation to NASA-MSFC Walt Wiesman set up several tours of the huge campus-like center for me. I visited the design and manufacturing labs first. Then came the "Clean Room," completely sanitized for making and joining sensitive parts. I also watched astronauts practice activities in simulated neutral gravity wearing scuba gear and weights in a tank of water. My guide said that Dr. von Braun came up with that idea himself. Rockets and boosters were tested by ingenious ways to imitate stresses of space flight. I saw giant "shake tables," like huge backyard swings with locomotive drive rods, mimicking the stress of launch.

Test

Most exciting was the test of the mighty F-1 rocket engine, still the most powerful one ever fired, five of which were clustered on the first stage of the Saturn V Moon Rocket. My tour guide, a fluent and personable engineer, showed me into a concrete bunker from which we would watch the action through a narrow slit in the thick wall of the bunker. In our line of sight through the slit was a towering test stand erected on the Alabama soil. It held in place the mighty engine, embracing it in its way. The rocket blast would roll off a special metal deflector at a 35-degree angle. Cold water began to flow down the shields and deflector during the ignition countdown. My guide explained that this would prevent the stand from melting. I asked him to explain the blast in terms a layperson could understand.

"Think of a rocket engine as a kind of controlled and continuous explosion," he said. It made sense to me, a word man.

The explosion was the loudest sound I have ever heard: 1,500,000 pounds of thrust from one engine. That is, One Million, Five Hundred Thousand pounds of thrust. As the flames hit the cold, running water a vast cloud of steam engulfed the stand; enormous clouds of smoke and steam roiled skyward. Trees located several hundred yards away bent over backwards from the shock waves. Then the roar abruptly ceased.

"Why didn't the rocket engine launch the test stand?" I asked my guide.

"It's the difference between starting to tow a car with a chain that is either slack or taut. We do not allow the engine to lunge at or away from the test stand."

I thanked my guide profusely as he drove me back to my building. I am sorry I did not remember his name. I felt privileged then to be privy to the rocket test and still do. I challenge the reader to interpret this example of a rocket engine test, to place it in the context of the larger themes of this book. It is central to those themes and I shall return to it after completing a narrative and explanation of my main research project.

I did some reading about the history of the organization's personnel and some listening to oral history. After von Braun and his associates surrendered—against Nazi orders—to the U.S. Army, they were sent to Texas and New Mexico without much to do other than test, test, test their old rockets. Dr. von Braun called this period their years of wandering in the desert.

As the Cold War heated up in 1950, they were sent to the U.S. Army Redstone Arsenal in Redstone, Alabama. The Arsenal Concept used by the U.S. Army made it the most effective and efficient of the major services. The U.S. Air Force, for example, did all their R & D and manufacturing with defense contractors. The Army, by comparison, did its own Research and Development and manufactured samples of weapon systems. This gave them an in-house "Yardstick" capability by which to evaluate the products turned out by defense contractors. The von Braun group developed our arsenal of intercontinental ballistic missiles by which we held the Soviet Union at bay.

When President Eisenhower signed the National Aeronautics and Space Act in 1958, von Braun and his organization made it clear they would prefer to move to NASA for their first love: making rockets for the exploration of Space. They moved into the new Marshall Space Flight Center in Huntsville, in 1960. They were given the job of doing the R & D for the Moon Rocket. Unfortunately, the Head of NASA at that time, James E. Webb, believed in the "Contract State," i.e., letting industry do the R & D and the manufacturing of finished products specified by NASA. This policy was widely criticized because it would leave NASA without the "Yardstick" by which to evaluate the goods manufactured for them. This created a tension between NASA Headquarters and the Marshall Space Flight Center: The Yardstick vs. The Contract State.

Compounding this was the development of resentment against the Paperclip Group, the Germans. My own mentor of younger days, Bruce Kendall, still had the feeling that they were the Nazis, the enemy who tried to kill him in London with the V-2. I understand the war mentality and I did what research I could and interrogated Walter Wiesman about the degree of von Braun's commitment to the evil regime and system. What Walt told me could be verified by research. Dr. von Braun directed R & D at the Rocket Center, Peenemunde on the Baltic, a place chosen in part so they could test missiles by firing them into the Baltic Sea.

It is clear from photographs I have seen that von Braun had to join the Nazi Party and wear the swastika. I believe that he had to join the SS as well, but there is no evidence he believed in the values of that organization. Indeed, it is well documented, and verified by Wiesman for me, that von Braun was placed in prison by Heinrich Himmler, the Head of the SS, second in command to Adolph Hitler. The charge or reason given was "Defeatism." I have heard two versions of what actions on his part fit the crime and imprisonment: (1) Dr. von Braun was quoted as saying that he would rather be firing rockets into the heavens than . . . .; (2) von Braun was quoted as saying the V-2s were coming down on the wrong planet. Either one makes me believe he did not believe in Nazism and Hitler's desire to achieve the conquest of Europe.

Another incident speaks highly of von Braun's own political beliefs. As what we call World War II was going against Germany from both the east and the west, von Braun was given an order to stand to the last man in defending Peenemunde against the advancing troops of the U.S.S.R. Instead of repeating the command to his own rocket scientists and engineers, Dr. von Braun showed something of a democratic streak by calling together the top technical personnel and put the question to them: What should we do?

What my sources related to me was that the unifying sentiment of these brilliant rocket scientists and engineers was this: Collectively the Peenemunde personnel were enthusiastic in articulating that they had had enough of working and living in a totalitarian system. This clearly shows they wanted to avoid surrendering to the Soviet forces and living within their system. They voted to disobey orders so that they could surrender to the American forces looking for them. This American group was headed by Colonel Ludi Toftoy, Head of the group called Operation Paperclip. They were known to be in Southern Germany.

My friend Walter Wiesman was chosen to commandeer a railroad train, pack it with blueprints and other objects important to rocketry, take on the personnel who then did travel south where they met up with the group under Colonel Toftoy. They were interrogated at length, and only those who were judged *not* to be "True Believers" in the Nazi system and had something to contribute to rocketry in the U.S. were selected. The number selected is captured in the title of their group: "Paperclip 120." I also heard a story told me by a couple of the Germans that during their interrogation, IBM representatives were permitted to sit in and take notes. Why would they have been interested? My sources said that the Germans had experimented with computers and had made some significant advances.

I learned from some Germans that there was a rocket scientist at Peenemunde who aspired to replace von Braun as the leader. He decided to stay and surrender to the Soviet forces. He was taken back to the U.S.S.R. But instead of giving him and others a lifetime job, they drained them of all their knowledge and sent them back to postwar Germany.

Rocketry, Music, and Theology

What did I know when I neared my first appointment with the Director, Dr. Wernher von Braun? I knew enough to be nervous. Over the years I have used a short list of his youthful accomplishments: By the age of 22, von Braun had two engineering degrees, a doctorate in Physics, a pilot's license. He knew three languages: German, French, English. The title of his doctoral dissertation was rather vague, something like "On Explosions," and was, of course, about rocket engines. He had the build of an NFL fullback or linebacker, was athletic, enjoying mountain climbing as a sport. I suppose I should add that he was handsome and in previous books about him and the space program, I used quotes from American authors who emphasized his "charisma," a concept developed by another German, Max Weber. His "Ideal Type" or abstract model specified that such characters are revolutionary.

Two Anecdotes

More about von Braun can be found in the book mentioned above, *Organizational Communication Imperatives* and a second book about three crucial incidents in NASA history: *Apollo, Challenger, and Columbia: The Decline of the Space Program (2005*). Let me, however, relate a couple of my favorite anecdotes. During my orientation I was shown the Space Center's Museum, full of historical items. There was another room, under lock and key, containing material that made von Braun a bit embarrassed because they were personal and highly laudatory. But Walt Wiesman, now a good friend of mine, had the key and let me in.

I will mention only one item: correspondence between Dr. von Braun and Dr. Albert Schweitzer. There was one exchange of letters in the German language initiated by Dr. von Braun after arriving in the U.S.A. I read the translation of both letters into my language. Schweitzer was a German with degrees and accomplishments in Medicine, Music, Philosophy, and Theology. Von Braun wrote that he had long appreciated Dr. Schweitzer's record in Music, Theology, and Medicine. He provided some autobiographical material and then wrote that he was now working in the U.S. for NASA, developing the equipment by which to explore outer space. He said that Science had taught him that nothing ever disappears. They can only be transformed. He added that he believed that this was true about human life, making a case for afterlife. He invited Dr. Schweitzer to visit the Marshall Space Flight Center, saying that there was an airport in Huntsville.

Dr. Schweitzer's reply thanked him for the letter, said it was unnecessary for Braun to explain who he is and where he is. He wrote that he had followed Braun's career closely. As to the question about afterlife, he said there was no room for it in his theology. He said he could not leave his medical camp in Africa, but he added that there was a landing strip near his medical compound where Braun could land for a visit.

The second incident was related to me by Wiesman that took place in Huntsville. The German crew had deeply influenced the culture of their town in Alabama. A quartet of space scientists playing music expanded until it became the community Orchestra playing classical music. They invited Arthur Fiedler and the famous Boston Pops Orchestra to play a concert in Huntsville. The invitation was accepted and when they arrived Walt Wiesman offered to show Fiedler around the Space Center, culminating with an interview with Director von Braun.

Walter told me that while he was giving the tour of the center, Fiedler confessed that he was getting quite nervous about the appointment with the Director.

"Why?"

"Because I don't know which end of a rocket to light," answered the Maestro. Perhaps part of that tension was due to the fact Fiedler's parents were Jewish immigrants from Austria.

"Oh, don't worry," said Walt, adding that things would go well.

Walt delivered the visitor to the Director's office and Fiedler was warmly welcomed. After a brief conversation, a piano and cello were brought into the office. The host explained that while he was working on his doctorate at the University of Berlin, he had taken a course in musical theory taught by a recognized German composer, Paul Handmith. He then pulled out some of his own compositions that could be played by a duet.

Wernher von Braun was one of the two most brilliant men I have ever met. The other has been mentioned several times in this book: KB or Kenneth Burke was a word man who wrote a small library of books about new developments in Rhetoric, Literature, and Philosophy, among other disciplines. WvB appreciated the arts and sciences and was able to envision and implement the machines delivering the future.

Organization Chart as Map and Geometry of Communication

I got a copy of the organization chart from Walt that is shown in Figure 1. I memorized it in no time because of its importance. In my doctoral training at Purdue Professor Redding had taught me that the vertical lines of authority are the formal communication channels. Orders come down the line, feedback and results go up—to simplify matters. Or as folk sayings have it, "good news goes up the line, bad news comes down." The lines on the chart represent the *formal* channels of communication; the informal lines of communication are *not* represented and thus their importance is underrated. An example might be two men at different levels of the hierarchy might be neighbors and fall into conversation about work that could be useful to both. Von Braun, I would discover, turned informal lines into quasi-formal and visible lines, as we shall see.

NATIONAL AERONAUTICS AND SPACE ADMINISTRATION

GEORGE C. MARSHALL SPACE FLIGHT CENTER

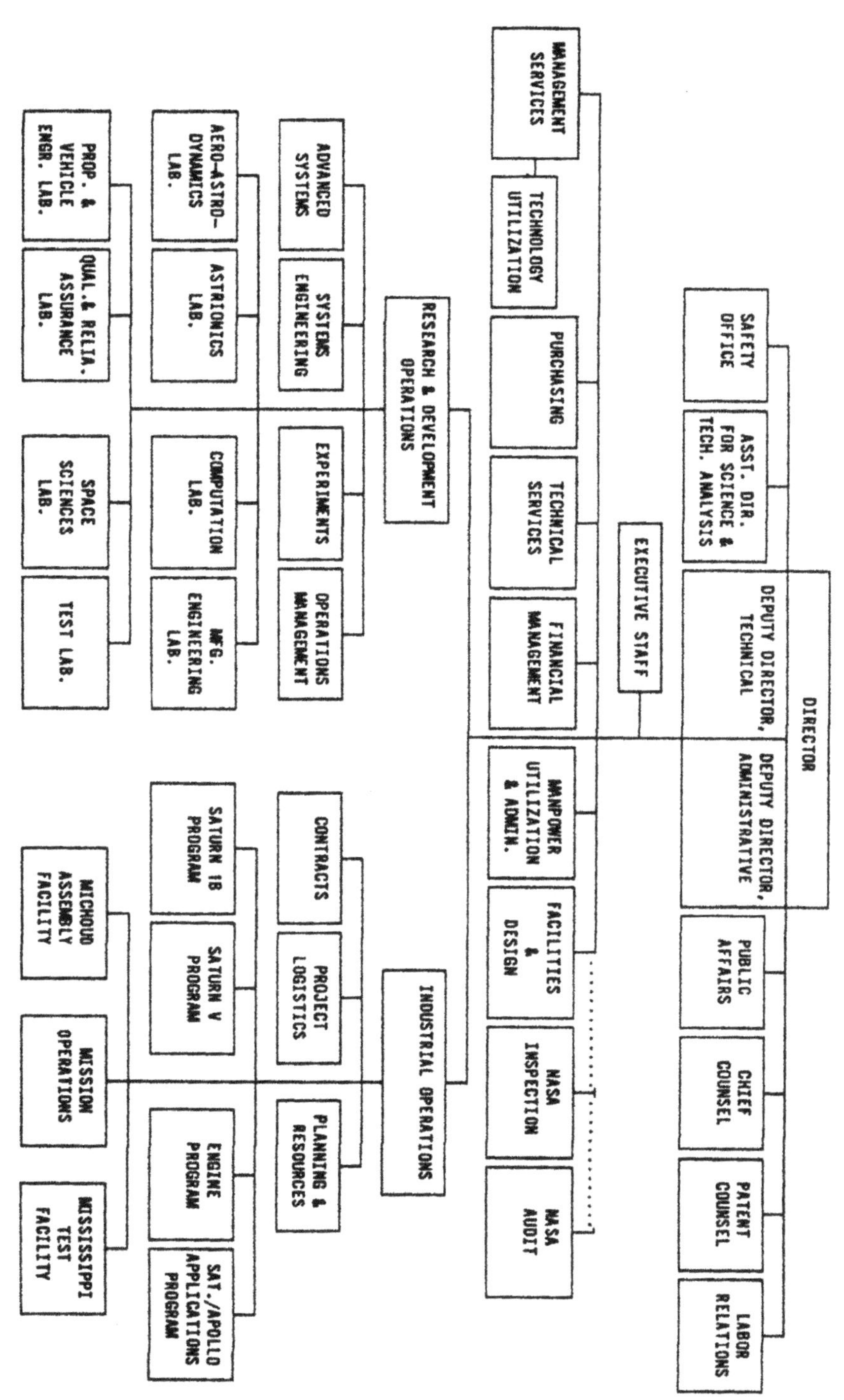

The reader is now encouraged to look with me at the Marshall Space Flight Center, or MSFC, chart in Figure 1. At the top of the highest box is the "Director," and it was filled by the most brilliant rocket scientist of all time: Dr. Wernher von Braun. His subordinates were, on the left, Deputy Director, Technical and on the right, Deputy Director, Administrative. The DD Technical was filled then by Dr. Eberhard Rees, the oldest of the German Paperclip 120. I learned he was called "Papa Rees" because of his age and unlike his younger boss, he felt free to bark commands to those below. On the horizontal lines were staff offices the top three could call on for advice on "Labor Relations," "Safety," and "Chief Counsel," a legal officer. Below them are another nine staff officers the three top people could draw on for help. The box in which I was located is Manpower Utilization and Administration, providing services such as Wiesman's internal communication experts, trying to educate the RDO and IO people and monitor results.

Then the organization divides into two main parts, Research & Development Operations, or R&DO, on the left and Industrial Operations on the right, or IO. I was surprised by the size of IO because I did not realize how much work on the Saturn V was done by independent contractors. That means complex lines of communication not represented on the chart, and lines of communication with other organizations such as contractors. More about the uniqueness of NASA-MSFC's relationships with contractors as we move on. This was an important part of my understanding and research at this complex organization chart-communication system.

On the left is R&DO. It is made up of the engineering and scientific disciplines necessary to do the research and development for a Moon Rocket. Advanced Systems looked to the future and tried to help the work at the then-backward present time. The other labs focused on different everyday problems to be solved: Notice the box for Astrionics, the Space Age name for electrical engineering. Propulsion and Vehicle Engineering designed engines, designing the best shape and structure to soar to the heavens. Notice there is a Test Lab, a unit that would grow in importance as I got deeper into the R&D of the Saturn V.

The Tompkins Diagnostic Study

After my reading and orientation period a couple of profound feelings came over me. The first was the commanding and attracting *presence* of von Braun. I could sense it in the way people talked about him, told me how thoughtful he was. I analyzed it as partly charisma, and partly Aristotle's form of persuasive proof: "*ethos.*" Today we translate that word, ethos, as "credibility," and it is a powerful resource in persuasion. The second feeling was one I discovered when I caught myself using the collective pronoun, the "we" of identity in reference to the Space Center: "Oh, I see, we do it this way, eh?" I had persuaded myself somewhat unconsciously to identify with MSFC closely and NASA to a lesser degree. It became part of my personal identity—yes, a significant part of Phillip K. Tompkins—ever since those days. Others acknowledge my NASA experience as part of my identity. I will refer later to the effect this identification would have on my own scholarly and subsequent research efforts in which I drew on the work of Kenneth Burke.

After my orientation period was completed, a week or ten days, I was given an appointment with the Director in his office. Although I felt some of the nervousness of Arthur Fiedler, being thirty-three-years old, an Associate Professor as I was, the differences were a) I was not the son of Austrian Jews; and b) I did by now know which end of a rocket to light. Walt Wiesman walked me over to the Director's office. After introducing me to von Braun, Walt turned to walk away.

Von Braun gave a loud order for him to join us, adding "Don't be so goddam lazy."

An administrative assistant to the Director named Jim Shepherd and the kidnapped Walt Wiesman sat in on the conference. Dr. von Braun spoke to me about the importance of communication, emphasizing upward-directed communication from people two or three levels down. That was unusual for a government bureaucracy because they limited direct upward comments to one formal level. He explained that MSFC was different, because it was "like being in the earthquake prediction business. You put your sensors out there and learn how to read them." It was a learned lecture with Tompkins taking copious notes.

He went on to my assignment. He asked me to interview the top 24 managers in the RDO and IO branches. Other interviewees were added later, adding up to about 45 to 50. He asked me to find out which communication practices "worked well, and those that do not work well."

My graduate work at Purdue University had included three graduate classes in Inferential Statistics, two of which got credit in Mathematics as well because the Professor was a member of both the Math and Psychology Departments. I was prepared to develop a standard written questionnaire to administer, but Wiesman later told me that someone had tried to survey the same population recently via a written questionnaire that the subjects complained loudly about because it stifled elaboration on complex topics. Von Braun and Wiesman both wanted me to use in-depth interviews of at least sixty minutes.

I prepared my Interview Guide with questions to open the rocket experts up, to get them feeling free to speak to me before posing the more important qualitative items such as what works and what does not. Dr. von Braun wrote a letter to every one of my interviewees, telling them how important it was *to tell the truth* to Dr. Tompkins. He wrote that their answers would be confidential, grouped without mentioning the names of who said what. The secretaries in Manpower made the telephone calls to set up the dates and times for my interviews. They said it was clear that they, the interviewees looked forward to my visit, had made notes to guide them in telling me what practices worked well and which did not.

Problems: What Did Not Work Well?

Readers of this book who would like to understand all ten problems I discovered via interviews in detail, plus my recommendations to solve or mitigate them can refer to my two Space books: *Organizational Communication Imperatives: Lessons of the Space Program* (1993) and *Apollo, Challenger, and Columbia: The Decline of the Space Program* (2005). Here I shall mention only one. The third item I reported in my briefing to von Braun was: "The Invisibility of the Boss." There was some nostalgia in this topic among those who remembered quieter days working for the U.S. Army when one could walk across the hall and chat with the Director. In addition, the size of the Apollo Project made it necessary for Director von Braun to attend meetings in the Washington, D.C. Headquarters of NASA, then fly to California to visit with contractors building parts for the Saturn V. My recommendation for this communication problem was to acknowledge that it was without a perfect solution, but I had also learned how much the engineers, scientists, and staff workers loved a von Braun visit to a lab or a staff office. There are photographs of him in labs, examining a part with a group around him. They could also let their members make short presentations for him. I also mentioned that many MSFC members were worried about their fate after the completion of the Moon Project. Would there still be a job and a mission for them? I recommended that von Bran set aside a time when the whole of MSFC could gather for a speech about their future. I was not surprised when the Director made a special note about that item and later gave the Center-wide speech.

The Director gave his complete attention to the problems and was eager to hear my recommendations. I emphasized that I requested and got recommendations from the interviewees. Now I move on to the more important findings, i.e., what communication practices constituted what I chose to call, with capital letters, Open Communication.

What Communication Practices Worked Well: Open Communication

Those practices that worked well relate more closely to the theme of this book.

Automatic Responsibility

I could hardly believe this when the managers with engineering and other skills told me about it. It was a practice, a principle that was drilled into every one of the 7,200 employees at the time. It went like this: If you discover a problem about which you have technical knowledge, the moment at which you *perceive* it you assume responsibility automatically for it, for solving it and sending the problem and solution up the line. If you recognize it as a problem but do not know how to solve it, you must communicate it up the line to the Director.

The interviewees gave me examples of it. I still remember one example when a young engineer realized he himself had made a mistake, a serious one, and sent word of his failure immediately up the line. Dr. von Braun sent him a bottle of champagne. I understood it because by then I had developed that deep degree of identification with NASA MSFC. I respected their goal of reaching the Moon and returning Astronauts safely to the Earth. I identified with the organization during my orientation and the first evidence I had was when I caught myself referring to the Marshall Center with a collective "we." It increased even with my understanding of being completely captured. Most organizations have difficulty in generating that degree of identification and commitment. It affected me so deeply that after I returned to the academic realm, I began a research program in organizational identification, getting outstanding graduate students at Purdue University and the University of Colorado to do research into the concept, drawing on the insights discovered by the Nobel Laureate, Herbert Simon, and the brilliant humanist, Kenneth Burke.

I should add that many management theories of the time tried to find solutions to employees who are indifferent about the success of their employers—but came up with nothing so powerful as Automatic Responsibility.

Penetration

When I put the word Penetration on the blackboard during classroom lectures, I could be sure to look back at smiling, giggling, sexually sensitive students. No, this is a different kind of penetration I would explain in this way: After von Braun and his 120 German rocket experts surrendered to the U.S. Army, they were taken to the

United States and eventually wound up working at developing rockets for the U.S. Army. Von Braun and his men were happy to settle into the Army's way known as the Arsenal Concept. That concept meant that the Army believed it was vital to have the engineering capacity to do the research and development necessary to come up with its own weapons, and only then released the plans to contractors to mass produce them. The Paperclip 120 were put to work doing the R&D for the intercontinental ballistic missiles that kept our Cold War enemy, the Soviet Union, from attacking us. When President Eisenhower founded NASA in 1958 as an independent civilian agency, von Braun and his team volunteered to join it. They became part of NASA, got an objective from President Kennedy to send a man to the Moon and back during the decade of the sixties.

The Paperclip group took the Arsenal Concept with them to NASA. While I was beginning my research in 1967, I found a book published a year earlier by an author named H.L. Nieburg. The book was *In the Name of Science* (Quadrangle Books), a tome about how some government agencies bought finished goods from contractors that did not measure up to worthwhile standards. Nieburg called it the Contract State, a phrase of disrespect. He praised von Braun by quoting him. It seems that von Braun was called up to Washington D.C. to testify before a Congressional hearing about problems with the Contract State. He was asked why his organization, the U.S. Army at that time, got a much higher quality of work done by contractors than any of the other government agencies, e.g., the Air Force and Navy, were able to receive. How do you do it?

Von Braun said he could answer the question in a word: "Penetration." He explained that his expert engineers did the research and development work for the missile or rocket. Throughout that process of R&D, they tested, tested, tested. Then and only then did they put the serial manufacturing up for bids. The company winning the bid would then be penetrated by von Braun's experts. The MSFC engineers would enter the factories, observe and talk to the contractor personnel, even their frontline workers, as they went about their business. They developed such trust that they could ask them about problems they encountered. There is a story that I have written about in which a contractor for the Saturn V rocket delivered their first make of the second stage of the Moon Rocket to MSFC in Huntsville. It had such high technical requirements that this stage should be a virtual vacuum. The MSFC crew asked the contractors how many cracks were in the stage.

"None," said the contractors.

"Yes, there are cracks. How many?"

"Twenty-one," was the answer.

"No," there are 26."

"No, only 21," and this time the contractor was *adamant.*

The MSFC personnel suggested that they submit it to an examination, a test involving an X-Ray. The findings were, yes, 26 cracks, plus a few workers' tools and lunch boxes inside the stage. The NASA engineers had penetrated the contractor, talked to contractor personnel, could both see and hear about the problems with the stage. That story made me proud, that we could insist on entering the plants and get to know the employees well enough to be trusted as expert advisers. It was suggested that in many cases the contractor employees felt better, safer in reporting problems to the Marshall Center penetrators than to their own superiors.

I wish each generation of government agencies dealing with contractors would practice penetration as effectively as NASA MSFC did back in those glory days. But now we turn to the most powerful and creative communication practice I have ever discovered. In October of 2019 I participated in a long, one-day conference celebrating the 50th Anniversary of the Apollo Program at Wichita State University, in my hometown. Most of the other papers were about technical aspects; my paper stood out because it was about a communication practice. Indeed, the claim in my title was that I was concentrating on the "Secret of Success" of the Apollo Project.

The Monday Notes

I have written more extensively about this marvelous practice, in *Communication Monographs* and in my two Space books: *Communication Imperatives: Lessons of the Space Program* (1993) and *Apollo, Challenger, and Columbia: The Decline of the Space Program (2005).* Here I give it a slightly new interpretation. But first let us look at how it developed and how it worked.

The answer I got in my interviews to the question of "What works well?" invariably was "The Monday Notes." The Monday Notes came into existence during the growth days of the Marshall Center. Kurt Debus, one of the "Peenemunde Gang," as von Braun called them, had always been the man in charge of Launch Operations for the organization. During a period in which Debus was away at Cape Canaveral supervising launches, von Braun felt that the lack of propinquity diminished vital communication between the two of them. He asked Debus to send him a weekly, one-page note from the Cape, in which he would describe problems and progress of the previous seven days.

Finding that he looked forward to reading the weekly note, von Braun decided that a similar note from other key personnel would help him keep informed and get important issues out in the open. He asked about two-dozen managers (all of whom I interviewed), lab directors in RDO and managers in IO who were removed from him by one layer of management, to send him a weekly, one-page note summarizing the problems encountered and progress made during the week. Simplicity was the key. There was no form to be filled out. The simple requirements were these: No more than one page headed by the date and the name of the contributor. They were due in von Braun's office each Monday morning. In this way a layer of management was bypassed on the way up, the Directors of IO and RDO; they could read the notes but could not change them in any way.

As von Braun read each note, he initialed it with a "B" in the right-hand top corner and wrote the date in numbers. (The first time I saw a set of the notes, the teacher in me automatically flipped through them looking for an "A" paper, a story that got big laughs at MSFC.) He also added a considerable amount of marginalia in his impeccably clear handwriting, making suggestions and dishing out praise. The notes of July 10, 1967, for example, include a hand-written question directed to a manager about vehicle cost figures included in his note: "Have we passed this on to Mueller [NASA Headquarters official]? B." There is a suggestion to another manager that a new computer mentioned in his note "could be immensely useful for earth resources survey from orbit. B." To a lab director whose earlier recommendations about the superiority of one type of weld over another had been rejected and who had conducted additional tests supporting his original position, von Braun wrote, "Looks like you won after all! Congrats. B" (Note: the additional tests must have included replications.)

All twenty-four notes were annotated and then collected in alphabetical order by each author's last name; they were then reproduced and returned as a package to *all contributors*. What was the organizational effect of this simple, innovative activity? I put that question to all contributors as I interviewed them. The answer was an unqualified praise for the notes. The reasons offered are worth considering.

The first virtue is obvious. The Notes served as one more channel—24 lines of communication—in addition to briefings and memoranda, to keep the boss informed with problems and progress. Whereas many organizations suppress bad news, this one sought it. It thus fostered another factor in the ideal managerial climate—openness and candor. Another benefit I learned was the crucial lateral or horizontal function of communication. Each lab director learned what all the other laboratories had been up to during the previous week; in addition, units in IO could read about the activities in RDO, and vice versa, which often stimulated additional horizontal interaction among them to maintain coordination of projects. A good illustration of this occurred during the interview process. A lab director I was interviewing said that the recently returned

Monday Notes contained a comment from von Braun suggesting that he needed to telephone a project manager in IO about a mutual problem. By chance, my next interview happened to be with that very project manager. Without prompting from me he volunteered that he had discovered a suggestion in the Notes that he needed to communicate with the lab director whose office I had left minutes earlier.

The marginalia supplied by the charismatic von Braun made Monday Notes the "the most diligently read document" at MSFC as a lab director said to me in an interview. This crucial *feedback function* was mentioned by nearly every contributor. They saw how the boss reacted to the week's work in their own units as well as his response to other contributors' notes. Another desirable effect mentioned by most of the interviewees was closely related to the feedback function. Because von Braun found it increasingly necessary to travel to California, the Cape, Washington, D.C., and other locations, the Monday Notes "kept the channels open" during the periods of limited face-to-face interaction.

The Notes were also an antidote to the sterile, formalized procedures that permeated government work period. Contributors derived a high degree of communication satisfaction from the *personalized* nature of the Notes, a break from the code-numbered-US Government-NASA-MSFC format designating the lab or office from which it emanated. Just the name and date at the top of the page. The contributors also derived what W. Charles Redding in his teachings called "communication satisfaction" from the *informality*, *quickness*, and *frankness* of the Notes. As to frankness, some rather fierce arguments were carried out in the Notes. One unit's note of the current week might challenge a note of a previous week by another unit. This controversy, said a lab director, gave the notes their particular "charm." Another lab director said with a disingenuous smile, "We sometime misuse them—to get attention." *The two-by-four and the mule again*, I thought. In other words, you knock the mule in the head to get its attention. The Notes provided a *public forum* and the *court of last resort*.

During my interviews I discovered something von Braun and the others did not realize. Curious about how the 24 contributors generated the contents of their weekly note, I systematically asked about their procedures. In most cases the lab director would ask his subordinates, the division chiefs, to provide him with a Friday Note about their activities. Von Braun was delighted to learn of this unexpected dividend when I briefed him later in the summer. (During the summer of 1968, I had the opportunity to interview 14 division chiefs. Most of them requested a similar note from their subordinates, branch chiefs, and so on.)

Moreover, some of the directors and managers organized meetings to determine what should be put in the next week's note and to discuss von Braun's responses to the most recent notes. Relevant portions of the Notes were reproduced for distribution down the line. In short, von Braun's simple plan for a weekly note had *generated a rigorous and regularly recurring discipline of Open Communication within the organization.* Once a week almost every supervisor in the organization paused, stopped what they were doing in order to reflect on what needed to be communicated *up the line*. Lab directors and project managers stopped to read what their peers had communicated to the Director and how he responded.

The Monday Notes also illustrate two general principles in von Braun's philosophy of organizational communication—*conflict and redundancy*—that were manifested in other ways as well. As indicated above, some rather heated conflicts surfaced in the Notes from time to time, as well as in briefings and memoranda. My interviewees sometimes tried to draw me into the conflicts in hopes I would advocate their side to von Braun. Occasionally I did, as when von Braun asked me to look at this or that controversy. Conflict was natural and necessary to such a large and complicated organization, and some of it was petty. Von Braun had a positive attitude toward conflict and sought to encourage it: perhaps he had even engineered the means to impress it into the very structure of the organization.

In my 2015 book, *Managing Risk and Complexity through Open Communication and Teamwork* (Purdue University Press), I quote and document a book chapter, "Learning in Organizations," written by Karl Weick and Susan Ashford, two organizational psychologists who had read my work on the Monday Notes. They described them as a model of organization learning and made other profound relevant statements.

After I briefed von Braun on the findings of my research, including the problems and recommendations, and what worked well, he jumped up, ran from his seat at the briefing table and got a big calendar from his desk. After the vigorous man studied it a bit he asked if I could come aback to Huntsville on a day in October. I agreed and he then asked me to give a two-hour briefing to the top 50 people at the space center. Dr. Von Braun wrote a letter to the President of Wayne State University asking him to give Dr. Tompkins the time to make the trip during the week to give an important report to his top Staff and Board meeting.

Reliability

The reader who has been observant about communication in organizations she or he has served, may have noticed this encouragement of upward-directed communication. This organization reversed the truism about most organizations: "Bad news comes down the line, good news goes up." That statement might even allow exaggeration and lying on what we want the boss to know. Look at the communication practices I discovered: Automatic Responsibility is focused on the solving and reporting upward problems. Penetration involves getting the facts at the bottom of a contractor organization and getting them up the line to the top of the customer's organization. The Monday Notes had upward communication skip a winnowing or straining layer of authority to maximize messages about problems and progress to the top. A story that I heard during my research illustrates the emphasis on the upward flow of information.

.99999s

Director von Braun was on one of his frequent trips to NASA Headquarters in Washington, D.C. During a group meeting one of the staff members asked:

"What is the reliability figure you have on the second stage of the Saturn V?"

"I don't remember it but when I get back to Huntsville, I will let you know."

After von Braun got back to the Marshall Center, he called the staff member in NASA Headquarters.

"I now have that reliability figure for the second stage of Saturn V: The staff member heard von Braun's answer to be "five nines," or "0.99999."

"Fine," said the HQ man, "How did you arrive at that number?"

"Well, first I called Walter Haeusserman, Director of the Astrionics Lab, and said "Walter is that second stage of Saturn V going to fail?" He said 'Nein.' I then called Karl Heimburg, the Director of the Test Lab and asked the same question. He said 'Nein,' and I kept at it until I had five Neins."

I drove back to Detroit and prepared my outline for a slide that would be magnified for the whole group. I was more than a bit nervous about talking for two hours to this group of brilliant rocket scientists about *their problems* I had diagnosed and *my recommendations* for improving them. I was interrupted time and again with questions and objections in a lively two-hour give and take. Dr. von Braun had introduced me and then told them that much of what I was going to say would be critical of them, the listeners. He asked that no one get up and leave the briefing room. Then he got a big laugh because, he said, he would have to miss the first part because of a phone call coming in from NASA Headquarters.

I began by mentioning the Monday Notes, as something they did well. When I concluded I moved to number 1 of the problems I would present. Before I could introduce it there was a question from the audience:

"Is that all we do well?"

"No," I snapped, "but I don't want you to feel too good at this point."

To the credit of my audience, they gave me a roaring, well-intentioned round of laughter. We went on, the Director joined us after his short absence, and I went through my list of ten recommendations for the problems we had generated. I was flattered by comments made to me at the conclusion. One American engineer said he heard one of the Germans say that "He knows us better than we know ourselves."

From that moment on I took the MSFC practices of communication as the ultimate standard. I began to distinguish it from most organizations by calling it Open Communication. As mentioned above, in 2015 the Purdue University Press published a book by P.K. Tompkins, the title of which is *The Management of Risk and Complexity through Open Communication and Teamwork*. It was not until this book began writing itself that I came to see that Open Communication was even more powerful when combined with Replication.

Replication in the Marshall Space Flight Center

In my previous articles and books, I did not talk about replication. I had encountered that method before NASA, in the Chemistry experiments and in the research for "In Cold Fact." It was not new to me when I began studying MSFC. But the communication practices were new and different from the standard theory and research in our new field of Organizational Communication. So, I stressed those communication practices and emphasized them by the expression "Open Communication."

The motivation for the book you are reading now is that by combining Open Communication and Replication, we have two methods for finding truth. So, for the first time I wish to show how this most successful organization used the practice of replication without a technical term for it. Let me list the applications I find in looking through my research in the summer of 1967 and 1968. Yes, I was asked to come back the next year as a Summer Faculty Consultant. I interviewed 14 people below the level of lab director for their problems and practices. I was also asked by von Braun to interview key members about what they thought the Space Center should concentrate on after the Apollo Project was complete, had achieved its magnificent goals. To what kind of space machines should they devote their bank of knowledge and skills after Apollo? One of the answers provoked a reaction from Dr. von Braun that would be prophetic, predictive of a profound tragedy—caused by the *absence of replication* in the form of tests. That will emerge in later chapters.

Let me list the applications of replication and its tragic absence numerically. This is not intended to be an exhaustive list.

1. When we looked at the MSFC organization chart, a prominent box in the Research and Development section was the Test Laboratory. They were experts in testing, organizing, conducting and evaluating them. Von Braun was famous as a tester, even infamous in some quarters for his frequent use of tests. I had observed, and *over*heard, a test described above, and I have no doubt that it was expensive to make that F-1 Rocket Engine test. The tests were often replicated and then replicated again with a slight change, a new complexity, or variable. Then a replication. It was so expensive and time consuming that NASA Headquarters imposed a restraint on von Braun and MSFC: "All-UP." My understanding of this order was that there could be tests of the three separate stages, but von Braun could not then, as he planned to do, test the first and second stages separately, then together and only then the all-up test. Nonetheless, von Braun was able to get enough tests in order to guarantee success. We made it to the Moon before the decade had ended, completely meeting the challenge of President John F. Kennedy. Let's call this category the Standard Replication. I will call the other test, with a new "variable," as Replication plus Variable.
2. Another category is called up by the Monday Notes. Recall the number of scientific and engineering specializations in the organization chart and in their Monday Notes. My daughter Emily Tompkins Lewis suggested that there were redundant reports, but from different angles or perspectives. That is, many reported success or failure, but with a different tongue or vocabulary pertaining to different parts or aspects. As my interviewees pointed out to me, there was another advantage of the Monday Notes: A single experiment, such as the F-1 engine I watched, provided what I shall call *Disciplinary* Replications. Dr. von Braun was a generalist as he watched a test, but he was slightly less learned in Astrionics, or electrical engineering, than the other disciplines. This problem was solved in part by having an Astrionics Laboratory reporting on tests. In addition, he heard several different perspectives on each test by the Propulsion Lab, Systems Engineering, Aero-Astro Dynamics, Space Science, and so on. By a slight stretch of imagination, one could say that a single experiment or test was technically replicated a dozen times in the Monday Notes. This made for a complex message to the readers, most importantly with the Director, but the competence of that consumer was never in doubt. Yes, the technical or disciplinary replications revealed a great deal to those at the top.
3. I did a bit of replication in 1968, repeating some questions about problems of communication, Monday Notes, penetration, and automatic responsibility.

    For the first time, I can say that the success of the Apollo Project was due to the combination of Replication and Open Communication. It provided the

Marshall Space Flight Center with the truth about the decisions they were making in the R&D of the Saturn V.

After the great success of Apollo, von Braun was kicked upstairs to NASA Headquarters. Then he went to work for a contractor and died at the age of 65. NASA went ahead with the Space Shuttle and we were all crushed with the disaster of the Challenger. I shall deal with the shuttles in later chapters.

In conclusion of this chapter, never have I heard of organizational communication that equaled or surpassed what I have just described. It has been presented as Open Communication. Now, for the first time I see and submit that Open Communication and Replication work together to provide the truth about technology.

Having stressed that new combination, I need to specify a couple of qualifications that will be important in the final chapter of this book. I must emphasize that Open Communication in MSFC was limited to a complex of organizations that created a new system.

Recall that I had to apply to the Federal Bureau of Investigation for a background check that gave me clearance to enter a partially secret enterprise. Yes, I was cleared because I had no connections to the Soviet Union and their space scientists and systems. All members of the organization had to have such clearance checks. We operated with the utmost in openness but also in secrecy with other countries and organizations.

The other qualification is that the Open communication is about topics related to achieving organizational success and avoiding failure. We can then say the two limits are systemic and purposive.

Open Book Management

No, I have to say, not every organization needs the Monday Notes. Why? Because not all of them must cope with such high risks—including human life—and complex objectives as did MSFC. Gary Moore, a friend who is introduced in the Addendum of the book, owned and managed an industrial supply company.

"In my industry there was a system called 'Open Book Management' . . . sharing as much relevant information in an organized way with everyone in the organization. That included essentially financial information. I supported and used most of the system" (e-mail, 1/25,21).

I did some research and found that credit for developing the system is given to John Case and his book: *Open-book Management: The Coming Business Revolution* (New York: Harper-Collins, 1995). Some of the basics of OBM are:

- Sharing financial and critical data about the company with employees.
- Employees are taught to keep score, helped to move numbers in ways that help the company.
- Employees should have a stake in the company and share in the prosperity.

Noteworthy is that my phrase for MSFC, Open Communication, and the name of the other stem, Open Book Management, both have the modifier "Open." Each must have some systemic limits on it.

Chapter Eight
Communication Crisis at Kent State: A Case Study and Connections

It is hard to realize how it was possible to teach classes, write academic articles, do the research for and publish "In Cold Fact" in *Esquire* magazine, do a major research study in NASA's biggest Space Center in preparation for the most successful Space launch, all within less time than three years as an Associate Professor of Speech at Wayne State University. These accomplishments were appreciated around the country but not by the Chairman of my Department. Ergo, I accepted an invitation to interview for a promotion at another university.

A Move to Kent State University

It was a feeling of accomplishment that aided me in accepting an invitation to interview for a job as Professor, or as academics say it to emphasize our top rank, as "Full Professor," at Kent State University in Kent, Ohio beginning in 1968. One of our top graduate students at Wayne State University, Carl Marcus Moore, had taken a job as an Instructor at KSU while he finished his dissertation. He told his colleagues there about my critical duel with Truman Capote, and more importantly, about my research and consulting role at NASA. Kent State University had no courses, no faculty in this increasingly important field called Organizational Communication. The Department Chairman at WSU had never said anything encouraging to me about my work and I was in my third year there.

The interview at KSU went extremely well. It was refreshing to be on a campus with trees and a green commons area called the "Quad," short for Quadrangle: a beautiful green contrast to the starkly city campus in downtown Detroit. A couple of members of the English Department at KSU showed up for my interview presentation. They later said they had heard about my visit and got a copy of my Curriculum Vitae, or academic resume', and discovered "In Cold Fact," and my article in the *James Joyce Quarterly* about the seventh episode of *Ulysses*.

Because the School of Speech, or they may have already changed to Speech Communication, was mainly interested in me as someone to introduce courses in Organizational Communication, I decided to lecture on the intricacies and complexities of the Monday Notes. As I spoke using a chalk version of the Marshall Space Flight Center organization chart as both my visual aid as my notes, I could see people in the audience busy taking notes, then asking questions, and at the conclusion, even the English department visitors complimented me about the lecture and encouraged me to take an offer from KSU seriously. They also mentioned an informal group that met in the evenings to translate collectively the learned and complex code in which James Joyce wrote *Finnegans Wake*. I returned to Detroit and waited for word from the Dean of the School of Speech Communication at KSU.

The offer did come with a promotion to Professor and a salary increase. I would begin in the fall of 1968 as a Professor. The word got around the discipline and I got some free advice. My former mentor from my M.A. thesis days and later, Bruce Kendall, had moved from the University of Nebraska to Purdue University and advised me strongly against taking the job. Why? Because it would make it more difficult to be readmitted to the more prestigious Big Ten. Maybe he knew that I had been invited to give a public lecture at the University of Wisconsin where he took his M.A. and Ph.D. I had not thought of it as an interview lecture, but much later learned that they were going to make me an offer to join their department at Madison, Wisconsin.

Bruce's advice did not influence my decision—so much for the prestige of the Big Ten, I said to myself-- and I accepted the KSU offer, and had a negative label applied to me by a key member of the Wisconsin department as a "Mover." The reader can no doubt grasp the negative connotations of the label. I told my colleagues at WSU about the offer and my decision. The only response from the Department Chairman was his request to have me make a copy of the letter that extended the offer. His reason was that he had heard that the fringe benefits were of such a nature that he should let his administrative superiors at Wayne State University know about them. To this day, however, I have respect for those Wayne State students for their ambition and discipline in both working and studying at the same time.

Transition

While teaching the spring term of 1968, my final term, in Detroit, I had a luncheon visit from a member of the faculty at Kent State, Associate Professor Bill Osborne and his wife Marty. I explained to them the complexity of the time between then and next fall. I had to pack up my stuff and send it to Kent, Ohio. Then I had to drive to Lawrence, Kansas to teach a short summer school course at the University of Kansas for the first time: Professor David Berg at KU had commissioned an article by me for the *Quarterly Journal of Speech*: "The Rhetorical Criticism of Non-Oratorical Forms." I would teach it for the first time, also make a quick trip to Wichita, Kansas to see my mother Phyllis Tompkins and other relatives. From there I would drive to Huntsville, Alabama to do some replications of studies done the year before, 1967, as well as some new probes. Then I would drive from Huntsville to Kent and move in.

I showed Bill and Marty my studio on floor 13 in Lafayette Towers and the few things I would need to move. Bill and Marty invited me to send them to their house in Hiram, Ohio, not far from Kent. They would store them until I arrived from Huntsville. They also offered to rent an apartment for me to move into.

Dr. von Braun had a lot for me to do and I wanted to interview some key people from the previous summer again for replication and thus increased confidence. I also, as mentioned above, interviewed people about the new directions in the U.S. Space Program, i.e., what kind of rocket could routinely send astronauts to the Space Station? It was only at the end of my interviewing program that I learned about Dr. von Braun's opposition to the proposed Space Shuttle, as mentioned earlier.

I told him that most of the rocketeers I interviewed wanted to make the Space Shuttle.

"We should never put human beings on a rocket powered by solid rocket fuels," said von Braun with quiet conviction.

"Why?"

"Because you can neither test them nor turn them off."

But as my readers know, the NASA officials in Washington, D.C., decided to go with the Space Shuttle, leading to two tragedies, Challenger and Columbia.

Tragedy at Kent State University

I was exhausted after driving from Detroit to my first summer job at the University of Kansas and my second job as a Summer Faculty Consultant at MSFC. It was hard to stay awake driving to my new apartment in my new home, Kent, Ohio. Then I had to get up the next morning to attend a Saturday morning meeting designed for me to meet and learn more about my new colleagues and for them to learn more about me, their new org com colleague. We had coffee and self-introductions around the table. Then we got off on topics of intellectual interest and I began to speak about my interpretations of rhetorical theory. Suddenly an attractive young woman rather fluently challenged my views, giving a different interpretation of the topic. We interacted for a while before our first break.

"Who was that?" I asked Carl Moore during that break.

"Elaine Anderson," he answered.

"Is she married?"

"Very."

I do not remember much about the rest of the orientation meeting other than my surreptitious observations of Elaine Anderson, adjusting to my disappointment.

Classes began the next Monday and I had no new preparations, but there was some disappointment because my first graduate seminar was in the rhetorical criticism of non-oratorical works. I got the message and so I offered the following term a basic graduate course in organizational communication to a big crowd. There was a high demand for this new field. The revolution was underway at Kent State. I found a new place to live and then turned to a new social life. Bill and Marty became good friends, took charge of my social life and introduced me to a couple of young women I dated.

The Kent state graduate students were attracted to basic theory and ate up my as-yet unpublished research at NASA. They loved the intricacy and beauty of the Monday Notes as I created them graphically on the blackboard.

They liked the idea of how replication worked, but neither I nor the students saw the connection to the Open Communication I taught them about NASA. I had not yet verbalized that the redundancy of the multiple notes on a single test provided a multiplication of the replication principle or Disciplinary Replication. They were intrigued with Penetration and Automatic Responsibility. We discussed how Automatic Responsibility could be psychologically *healthy* for those asked to practice it, offering people the key to open a door. They seemed to agree being willing to accept, even seek, rather than shirk responsibility was good for us.

I also shared with them the problems of communication I discovered at MSFC along with the recommendations made in my two-hour presentation to von Braun's Staff and Board Meeting.

I had also given the keynote address summarizing all empirical research in Organizational Communication in Walt Wiesman's convention on the subject in Huntsville. I supplied NASA with the manuscript of the presentation, and they published it. There was a high demand for those printed copies of my lecture until NASA wore out the stencil. The graduate students at Kent State University at that time were probably more advanced in knowledge in our topic than the students at perhaps any other program in the country. There is a record of how many of them I called on when it was necessary to ask them to do research interviews for me and the university when it happened.

I was writing this book on replication and truth when we came up to the 50th anniversary of the Kent State Shootings in 2020. My daughter Emily gave me her copy of the May 4 edition of *The New Yorker* magazine containing an essay-review of books about the event. It was written by the eminent Harvard historian Jill Lepore with the title "Blood on the Green." It refreshed my memories even though I had organized a study of the university and written a book immediately after it happened. It also brought back memories that jarred me into finding a parallel of those times with the now in 2020, or what people call the "new normal."

It happened in the spring of my second year at KSU. Kent State was not one of the radical campuses in the country where there were frequent demonstrations against the White House, President Nixon, and the Vietnamese War. There were protests on many campuses beginning in 1965 but no, we had not seen much of them on the KSU campus, with one exception I had forgotten. For many students, Kent State was considered a week-day school because so many students spent their weekends in other towns and cities. It was a quiet, conservative place. I seemed to fit in there because I had been brought up and educated as part of the "Silent Generation." That generation, or I should say *we*, were the people born between 1925 and 1945, a period of Depression and War. Born in 1933 I had also experienced the Dust Bowl, Depression and World War II. We are characterized as having a strong work ethic and proud national loyalty during World War II against those evil Fascist forces.

But then came an unhappy war, one that tested our allegiance. The Vietnam War involved the death and wounding of Americans who volunteered and were also drafted. I have seen a count as high as 47,000 deaths. And for what purpose? The North Vietnamese had not attacked Pearl Harbor, nor any other American territory. It was far away in miles, unimportant to an American's Existence until one was sent to *fight* the forces of the North. The war eroded loyalty and made young people a more questioning, critical and loud generation. Hope was seen earlier in 1970 when President Richard Nixon announced that he had decided the U.S. Government would start bringing home 150,000 American troops from Viet Nam. Young protestors thought they had been heard, but then ten days later, on Thursday, April 30, 1970, President Nixon announced on television he was making an "incursion" into Cambodia to attack North Vietnamese forces.

Thursday, April 30, 1970

I made a point of listening to the speech and knew instantly that it would not work rhetorically, hence politically, that we would be in trouble, even on a conservative campus such as Kent State. I knew that in part because KSU students had raised questions and complaints in my classes about the war. Their concerns were becoming more and more intense. I could not ethically defend the war because I did not believe in it. Know that during my boyhood I had saved money, pennies, nickels, and dimes to buy U.S. Stamps and War Bonds to help finance the war against Germany, Italy, and Japan. I was fiercely loyal to our American cause. But Nixon's "Incursion" speech failed to move me.

Timing of *The New Yorker*

As mentioned above, on May 4, 2020 the *New Yorker* magazine ran a five-page piece (70-75) by the prominent Harvard historian Jill Lepore, "Blood on the Green: Kent State and the war that never ended," a review of books about the aftermath of the KSU killings.

Lepore covers the action by using a block quotation from Hugh Downs' "grave, concise, newsman's account of the sequence of events" that he gave on NBC's "Today" show:

> On Thursday, April 30th, 1970, President Richard Nixon announced that American forces were moving into Cambodia. On Friday, May 1st, students at Kent State University in Kent, Ohio, expressed their displeasure at the President's announcement. That night there was violence in the streets of Kent. On Saturday, May 2nd, the R.O.T.C. building was burned, National Guardsmen moved onto the campus. On Sunday, May 3rd, students and Guardsmen traded insults, rocks, and tear gas. On Monday, May 4, the confrontation continued. There was marching and counter-marching. Students hurled rocks and Guardsmen chased students, firing tear gas. The Guardsmen pursued the students up an area called Blanket Hill. Some guardsmen pointed their rifles menacingly. And suddenly, it happened.

Other important events happened that are in that causal chain. As one example let me explain that the newly elected Mayor of Kent, Mr. LeRoy Satrom, knew no one, no administrators at the university he could call on Friday night after the violence downtown. Instead, he called Governor James A. Rhoades who was looking for some political action. He sent in the National Guard to the city and campus to prevent any more broken windows or bonfires.

On Monday, May 4 I went to my office early. It was too cool there to concentrate on grading a stack of student papers I needed to return to a class meeting that afternoon. So, I drove back home and did the grading in warmth and with classical music emanating from the turntable. I did not get to return the students' papers because classes were cancelled for the rest of the spring term. We had to conduct our classes via telephone and the U.S. Mail, what we now call remote learning after the coronavirus pandemic.

I did see a few students on campus before they went home. One of the students in an undergraduate course in Communication Theory I was teaching approached me on the quad with a question.

"May I give you a term paper without any words?"

"I don't know, John, I have never seen one before. Tell me what you have in mind."

"I was on campus that day with my camera. I took some black and white photographs that I can arrange to say something important about communication theory."

"Okay, John, go for it."

John gave me the "paper" in a file to hold the pages together. I "read" the wordless paper when I received it, a series of black and white photographs showing the two groups of protestors and Guardsmen facing off, the front rank of one group on one knee with rifles locked, loaded, and aimed at the student demonstrators. Then the photograph of a young woman, herself on one knee. She was close to the prone, face-down bleeding body of a young man. She has her hands reaching for the heavens, asking *why*? The look on her face is one of horror. Then photographs of more bloody bodies. The final shot is a young man with his finger pointed at a Guardsman, nonverbally saying "He did it."

I gave John an A+ for his paper and kept a copy of it. John was back in his hometown in Pennsylvania where he gave a copy of his paper to his local newspaper. They were so impressed with it that they nominated it for an honor. Yes, John P. Filo's term paper in my undergraduate course in communication theory won the Pulitzer Prize for Photography in 1970. While writing this chapter it occurred to me to raise a question to be answered by readers of this book: How many undergraduate term papers have won a Pulitzer Prize? John P. Filo would enter my life later to take some vitally important photographs.

Replication: An Organizational Communication Study of KSU

It was widely known on campus and in the administration building that I had done diagnostic studies for NASA's Apollo Project at the Marshall Space Flight Center, so I was appointed to the Kent State Commission to Study the causes of the disaster. This was important because some of the public at large seemed to think the National Guard had done the right thing.

"They should have shot . . . more of them," was a quote heard from many citizens opposed to demonstrations against the war. They supplied their own figures of persons shot, much higher than four dead and nine wounded. Students and other young people against the war and fearful of the draft were outraged. Some four out of five campuses across the country had demonstration against the incursion of Cambodia and the Kent State shootings. At the first meeting of the KSU Commission I was appointed Chair of a Committee on Communication. President Robert I. White also gave me a grant to subsidize my research project—even though I had never seen him, and never saw him after the shootings. I used it mainly to pay faculty and graduate students in the Division of Rhetoric and Communication to do interviews of their counterparts.

We drew a scientific sample of students, faculty, department chairs, deans and upper administrators. We did tests of questions until we developed a standardized interview guide for each group. We interviewed almost 500 people, and the guide in essence asked what worked and what did not.

Students had been banned from campus so we had to find them where they were, interviewing them in person when we could, but mainly on long distance phone calls. Those of us on the faculty were also doing long-distance teaching by mail and telephone to end the spring term. We thereby established a precedent for the faculty and students during the campus closings caused the coronavirus: remote teaching. Except—we did not have cellphones, computers with Zoom features, and other forms of modern communication.

Findings and Replications

Our report to the Commission was unanimously approved and sent to the President. It thoroughly criticized the President, Robert I. White, for not meeting his communication responsibilities. It was a replication of my NASA study only in the sense of method, not of phenomena studied. The cause of President White's failure during the crisis was traced to the routine practices of communication. He was invisible and uninformed by upward communication. He was the only administrator I could not interview because I could not get an appointment with him.

It was the opposite of the Open Communication found in the Marshall Space Flight Center. I had to use the principle of *replication* for several reasons while interviewing the members of the administration to confirm the unbelievable reports from my first interviewee. I had to interview *additional* administrators to confirm the assertions, to make sure I had the truth. In *addition*, I had to replicate interviews to get others to tell the truth in order to *protect the identity* of those early interviewees who feared they could have been identified by the President from their quotations, then singled out for some punitive action. A small number making critical remarks about the routine functions—and dysfunctions—of the organizational communication system might also have been traceable. To limit leakage, I did all of the interviews with administrators.

Here is the beginning of Chapter 7, "Conclusions," of *Communication Crisis at Kent State*:

> It seems conclusive to us that the disintegration of Kent State University during the crisis of May 1970, can be traced to certain organization-communication *imperatives* which were present in the routine functioning of the university: a highly centralized and indecisive administration which operated "blind" because of inadequate upward-directed communication; a President with little appreciation for his communication responsibilities; the absence of a two-way system of communication designed to integrate all segments of the rapidly expanded university; academic officers who were shut out of administrative decision-making; a fragmented, print-oriented faculty whose loyalty was to the department and discipline rather than to the university; large numbers of students who had been alienated from the university because of communication denial; and non-academic divisions which were found to be isolated from the academic sectors (p. 119).

These are the worst findings I ever reported in any study, nor can I remember reading a worse set of conclusions in a diagnostic study. The lack of open communication produced an even more astonishing set of facts. To follow, in a precise form, are the astonishing details I learned from those administrators I interviewed. On Friday, May 1, President White left town without informing *anyone* at the university. The Academic Vice President, the person formally expected to assume the President's responsibilities during his absence, was ill, bedridden and *unaware* that the President was gone. That means there was *no one* formally designated to negotiate with the new Mayor, nor the Governor, nor the National Guard officers. Decisions were made without the advice and consent of the university administrators responsible for doing so. The Vice President for Student Affairs tried to assume some responsibility by writing a memo, or flyer to be distributed on campus. He and an assistant began to write what would be the unretractable, unchangeable, and fatal position of Kent State University.

The Student Affairs Vice President relied on the recommendation of a member of his staff, a man with a law degree. The lawyer had experienced a conversation with some Guard officers and got the "impression" that the National Guard had decided, ordered, commanded that no more demonstrations would be allowed. The "flyer" they composed was placed in student mailboxes on Sunday, May 3, 1970; the message informed students—if any read it—that the right to assemble and protest had been stripped from them by the National Guard. How many students would look in a dormitory mailbox on a Sunday? Many must have read other signs that the gathering for the protest was to take place at noon. Whether planned or not, that means that many, many Kent State students would be crossing the Commons area, the Quad, on the way after class to lunch.

A Foolish Consistency

Another meeting was held by Guard officers with administrators that Monday morning. Interviews and press accounts said that *the Guard asked the university officials whether the protest gathering should be allowed.* This clearly implies the Guard leadership were willing to let the demonstration take place, even letting the administration make the *decision*—one way or the other. The administrators said that if they did not ban the meeting the decision would be inconsistent with the position on the flyer distributed to students earlier. What is that old saying? "A foolish consistency is the hobgoblin of small minds." But despite how striking that saying is, it is insufficient to describe the blood on the green that ensued.

The students were sent home after the shootings and slowly we tried to resume our educational process via the media of long distance available then. Elaine Anderson, the Instructor, did a masterful job of coding and summarizing the data from hundreds of interviews. Our report to the Commission was accepted with high praise. We decided to write a short book. I had no publisher and did not have time to seek one. An academic theorist of communication and psychology named Lee Thayer advised me to propose a book to Gordon and Breach Science Publishers. They agreed immediately. With Elaine's help I produced a typewritten manuscript of 160 pages. It was a first, or rough, draft and we waited and waited for the copy-edited manuscript to come back from the publisher. It did not arrive.

Instead, I received in the mail a couple of hardbound and paperback editions of a new book by Phillip K. Tompkins and Elaine Vanden Bout Anderson: *Communication Crisis at Kent State: A Case Study.* It included John P. Filo's black and white Pulitzer-winning photographs. Gordon and Breach had merely photographed the typewritten pages of the manuscript, a rough draft, published a few copies and then went out of business. That is why so few people ever heard of or saw a copy of that book. In addition, although we were horrified by the killings and can to this day not understand why the National Guard officer gave the order to fire and why the Guardsmen pulled the trigger, we had to attribute a large part of the *blame* to the administration of Kent State University.

I must amend a previous sentence, the one saying no one ever read the book. Someone must have read it. In 2016 I was informed by Routledge Publishers that they had plans to republish the little book, photographs and all, in a bright red hardback version of the original. They asked for our permission and we granted it, adding a question: Why are you publishing it again? The only answer we got was "We believe it should be in Libraries." They asked me for a foreword to the new edition. I wrote a page and one-half in which I responded to the view I heard from one reader that the criticism of the Kent State University was "harsh." We intended for it to be harsh, even at the risk of alienating anti-war protestors who wanted *all the blame* to be placed on the Guard and the Governor. We still deplore the foolish mistake of the KSU administrators, but we also mean to be harsh in our words about those who ordered the firing and the ones who pulled the trigger.

Aftermath

On May 14 of 1970, ten days after the Kent Sate killings, two students at Jackson State College, a black college in Mississippi, were killed and twelve were either wounded or injured. At Kent State we got the impression that the students were protesting both the war in Viet Nam and the killings at Kent State. In fact, people at KSU organized a Kent State-Jackson State Fund. Elaine Anderson and I designated a small percentage of our royalties to go to the KS-JS Fund. Alas, we never received such a royalty check. We clearly saw a connection between Kent State and Jackson State at the time.

People involved in the Fund were invited to a party in the front yard of the Virginia home of U.S. Senator Ted Kennedy. A reader said of the first draft of this book, "but he lived in Massachusetts." Yes, but he commuted to Washington from the home we visited. Music was provided by Gordon Lightfoot and a group of folk-rock musicians. Refreshments, food and wine were provided, and there was an appearance of the host. As Senator Ted Kennedy circulated among the guests, I realized that the crutch Elaine was using because of a recent auto accident might give Kennedy the impression that the youthful Instructor might be one of the nine wounded students. In fact, his eyes did expand as he approached us and focused on Elaine. I got myself into position to shake hands with him first and then introduce Elaine as a member of the faculty and my co-author of the book about Kent State.

Elaine Anderson had recently sued for divorce without opposition from her husband. We became something of an item because of the time we spent together working on the study and book. More about that later but I must add this block quote here:

> It is 12:23 p.m. on Monday May 4, 2020, as I type this line. I hope the reader may not find it an incredible coincidence, so powerful that there might be other unconscious forces at work that drew me to write this on the fiftieth anniversary of the Kent State University tragedy on Monday, May 4, 1970.

There was that scholarly work on the topic that appeared on the fiftieth anniversary: the article by Jill Lepore, mentioned above, that appeared in the *New Yorker* magazine on the same date: May 4, 2020. The article contained a summary by Hugh Downs of the Today show quoted earlier in this chapter. The title, again, is "Blood on the Green." Lepore is the author of twelve books and writes often for the *New Yorker*. This piece is an essay-review, an artful discussion of KSU and consequences, carried out by mentioning and quoting books about KSU save one.

She mentions that some think that the Kent State and Jackson State killings were related and responses to them are captured in her subtitle: "Kent State and the War that Never Ended." Some authors she cites did not see the connection, that Jackson State and subsequent demonstrations were strictly about race. She questions this interpretation, arguing that the subsequent protests on most campuses in the U.S. were a combination of animosity toward the Cambodian incursion and Viet Nam War, anger against the Kent State shooting, and against Racism and Police brutality. She would count the National Guard violence as related to police violence.

She supports her historian's thesis by drawing on her sources to establish that on May 7, three days after the Kent shooting, a sign was posted at Jackson State calling for a meeting to "discuss Cambodia." A small crowd showed up for that, but on May 9 about a dozen Jackson State students attended a rally in downtown Jackson, Mississippi. Lepore cites one of the books she was reviewing in this way, quoting one leader as saying: "The kids at Kent State had become second class niggers, so they had to go." They discussed how the Kent State students learned what happens "when the police think you're black."

The subtitle of her article, the "war that never ended," cannot be limited to Viet Nam because that war ended. Her article appeared on May 4; ergo, it could *not* have referred to the George Floyd murder on May 25, which stimulated massive national protesting of police racism populated by Whites as well as people of color. Further support for Lepore came from a scanning of the Tompkins-Anderson book.

I had forgotten that we had discussed Black protests prior to the May 4 demonstration-tragedy at KSU. In presenting a short history of Kent state we talked about how Kent State students were rather quiet in the late 1960s. On p. 5 a striking paragraph appears:

> But not completely quiet. On November 13, 1968, members of the Black United Students and the Students for a Democratic Society staged a sit-in to protest the presence of recruiters from the Oakland, California Police Department (long a bitter foe of the Black Panthers).

After the administration threatened punishment for the demonstration, 250 Black students walked off campus demanding amnesty. The incident makes me think that there were Black issues as well as the anti-war cause creating a national rhetorical movement. The Oakland Police demonstration can be linked with the Black Lives Matter Movement after the murder of George Floyd committed by a member of the Minneapolis Police Department: a war that has not ended.

By stimulating me to check our own comments fifty years ago, Historian Lepore enabled me to make some connections or continuities begun fifty years ago. Americans protesting President Nixon and the Viet Nam War combined with Racism to make a powerful energizer. We are still battling against Racism, a continuing, ongoing war.

Were the racially diverse protests of Police Racism in 2020 connected in a kind of replication from one city to another? I considered this idea and shared it with a good friend, Gregory Desilet, an ABD in Communication and Philosophy, and author of several scholarly books. He thought that I should make a clear distinction between replication and repetition. Or perhaps I should say mere repetition. I agree with him and will not call it replication. But I do see in the repetition of local movements a kind of acting out of truth or wisdom, the value of demonstrating against the unjustified taking of life. Those demonstrators must have experienced a profound sense of identification with previous and later participants. Let us call it a repetitive, common experience of the rhetorical call against injustice.

Open Communication Irony

There was a kind of conceptual replication between the two "what works and what doesn't" diagnostic studies I did at NASA and at KSU. The irony is that one would expect a university to be more open in its communication practices than a government agency, but that was not the case. Little or no upward communication in the university, even though the faculty have a higher status than most administrators. The universal pursuit of truth at a university—that Truman Capote did not seem to appreciate—should be more liberating than the R&D of a rocket. But it was not.

The saddest part of the tragedy for me is that the National Guard officers offered us, the university and its students, the right to assemble that day fifty years ago. We, represented by a minor official, rejected the offer because of the fear of making a minor misunderstanding. The result: Four dead in Ohio, and nine wounded.

Chapter Nine
A Honeymoon and More at SUNYA

It was in the early part of 1971 that I received an invitation to interview for a job at the State University of New York at Albany. They were going through the disciplinary revolution of changing from being a Department of Speech to a Department of Rhetoric and Communication. I did not know anybody in the Department, but a Dr. Kathleen Kendall invited me to make the visit and made the arrangements.

I was surprised by the architecture of SUNYA; it was a striking, all white one-piece campus, made of a large, one-story cement floor with columns and buildings growing up out of it. I heard that Edward Durrell Stone designed it for a place in India, lost the contract and sold it to the Rockefellers. New York was late in developing its state university, calling it SUNY with maybe sixty small campuses and four university centers, i.e., the latter having authority to grant a Ph.D. degree, one of which was SUNY Albany, the rest in Binghamton, Buffalo, and Stony Brook. I was directed to the Department office where I was met by Dr. Kendall.

"Good timing," she said with a smile, handing me the *Quarterly Journal of Speech, folded open to show an article,* "The Rhetorical Criticism of Non-Oratorical Works," written by Phillip K. Tompkins but seen by me at that moment for the first time in print. Inspired by the "In Cold Fact" case, I mentioned how rhetorical criticism could be used to unpack and understand literary works as well as orations, the mainstay of the Speech Field in the past. I thanked her giving me my first look at it.

Dr. Tompkins and Dr. Kendall became Phil and Kathy as she showed me around the department and introduced me to the faculty. The interview went well, I got an offer and I let them know that I was going to marry my recent co-author, Elaine V.B. Anderson, and they offered her the position as an Instructor in what would become the RCO Department. SUNYA they had an extra requirement as well. When we got there, Elaine and I would have to organize a communication study of SUNYA, a *replication* of the Kent State study. The purpose was to see if they needed to make changes in human relations between students, workers, and faculty to help with everyday problems as well as cope with the Viet Nam Protest Movement and other problems. I saw this as a great opportunity.

As a technical note, it would be a replication of the studies I had done at NASA and KSU, but quite obviously not a repetition of the phenomenon studied. The purpose was to find out if there were differences between the two universities. In the case of SUNYA, they hoped the results would be different from those produced by the KSU study.

Elaine and I got married on June 21, 1971 in the arboreal garden in the backyard of the home in which her mother and stepfather lived in Grand Rapids, Michigan. Graduate students from KSU attended and a Pulitzer Prize winning photographer presented us with a pictorial wedding present. We decided to camp out on a honeymoon that would take us up and around a couple of Great Lakes and into Canada to come back into the U.S. closer to Rapid City, South Dakota. In Rapid City we drove up to the home of Mr. and Mrs. John Lux. Jo Ann Lux had been Jo Ann Tompkins until our divorce in 1965. Kari Tompkins, aged nine, was eager to join Elaine and me in our campsite in the Black Hills. Eight-year-old Terry said no because as he said, "You look like a hippy," referring to my long hair, beard, and blue jeans.

His mother and stepfather brought him out later. He became fascinated with the campfire, feeding it carefully. Yes, later he did become an outstanding fire fighter with the U.S. Forest Service. The next morning Elaine took Terry with her to do some laundry and he said,

"You aren't mean like stepmothers in stories."

Missing was my fifteen-year-old son, Todd Phillip Tompkins. He was born with a diverse collection of birth defects that would not get a label until many years after his birth: Wolf-Hirschhorn Syndrome. Those curious about it can look it up. I will simply say that Todd was small, retarded and happy. Jo Ann had sent him to a State Home for the retarded before our visit. He would, years later, come to live in the wonderful Black Hills Workshop just outside Rapid City. Elaine and I took a tour led by the Director. Todd was part of the touring group and was greeted cheerfully at every stop in the huge building. He would contract the coronavirus at age 64 and survive it without pause. He is the happiest man I know, singing "Happy Birthday" to me nearly every time I talk to him on the phone, as he did last Saturday.

We drove south to visit my family in Wichita and then head east for Albany and a new university. It was later said of me by Professor Kendall that "Phil was very democratic, so we spent a lot of time in meetings." Yes, and we became the Department of Rhetoric and Communication, RCO for short. The big excitement came when it became known that academic administrators asked me to organize an organizational communication study of the SUNYA administration, like the one we had conducted at Kent State.

I asked faculty and students in the RCO Department to take part in the study, conducting interviews with a standard interview guide we adapted somewhat from KSU. I do not have a copy of the report we gave the administrators asking for the study, but we decided to add some theoretical questions that made for an academic article published four years later. We interviewed 319 people, a number that amazes me now because I, a newcomer organizing the study, had to get many faculty and students unknown to me to do the interviews.

The numbers broke down this way: Administrators (Pres., VPs, etc.) N=13; Directors (Library, Comp Center, etc.) =14; Deans (Colleges and Schools) N=11; Chairs N=19; Faculty N=74; Students N=123; Civil Service (Secretaries, Maintenance, etc.) N=29. What did they answer when asked about the communication system? In terms of a replication of the Kent State study, we got a different set of answers. We informed the administration that they were sensitive to upward communication. Thereafter they looked kindly on a department that brought good news. In switching from Speech to Rhetoric and Communication the enrollments went up and so did the number of academic positions for which we could recruit new members.

One of the freshmen students who took part by interviewing other students was named Michael Lampert. Watch for him again so that you can understand how he became a valued Research Associate on this project, this book on replication and open communication. Mike would take several courses from me and would teach me the political ropes at SUNYA. We gave the administration high marks for the routine functioning of their org com system: it did not, of course, approach the level of Open Communication I found in the Marshall Space Flight Center. But then as mentioned above, the purposes of the two organizations were different.

Several colleagues joined me in writing a paper about the large body of quantitative data, inspired by theory and gathered during the org com survey. We submitted it to *Speech Monographs*, a study of some of Kenneth Burke's philosophical and communication concepts. It took several years to get the data analyzed in the Computer Center, get it written, submitted and accepted in a journal that was going through its final year. Yes, in the same year the article was published in *Speech Monographs* the journal changed its name to *Communication Monographs*. Here is the full academic citation for this historic document:

> Phillip K. Tompkins, Jeanne Y. Fisher, Dominic A. Infante, and Elaine L. Tompkins, "Kenneth Burke and the Characteristics of Formal Organizations," *Speech Monographs*, Vol. 42, June 1975, pp. 135-142.

It was an accomplishment to reduce Burke's philosophic theory to a few terms, ask over 300 people to quantify those terms, and then do tests of statistical significance. Here are the philosophical terms as we presented them in the article on p. 135: "The current authors felt that Burke's work—with its key terms of *hierarchy, order, mystery,* and *identification*—could be applied to the study of organizational communication."

When I studied Burke's rhetorical theories, I understood the power of identification, but when I studied communication at NASA's Marshall Space Flight Center, I *saw and felt* the power of identification: Men who worked overtime without pay and with contractor personnel making much more in wages and overtime pay. Yes, I saw it and felt it and had the urge to begin researching it. We developed the first, albeit crude, quantitative measure of it, but our success led me to do and direct graduate student work on the topic.

Here are the concluding thoughts of the article:

> In conclusion, Burke's concepts of mystery and identification (and their "compensatory" relationship) seem to be confirmed by the quantitative data gathered in what we think to be the first empirical test in the real world.

There would be many more done by me and my graduate students.

RCO Department Grows

Elaine and I loved the university, department, and our new five-acre home in the foothills of what we called the Helderburg Mountains. We discovered that Stone's architecture was highly functional. The floor of the campus was one story above the ground, leaving a sheltered space underneath. During cold winter weather I could walk in sport coat or even shirt sleeves in the warm tunnels to meetings in other buildings or to the building where we could enjoy an excellent meal for lunch.

As mentioned above, our RCO courses drew more and more students. I took over RCO 100, an introductory mass lecture course at the freshman level, from Jeanne Fisher, so that she could work on her tenure and promotion case. I was able to double the number of students, or FTE's, as the accountants called them.

From a maximum of 100, I took in 200, then 300, and then I went too far with 400 in RCO 100. I assigned a short term-paper that I was still grading on Christmas Eve. Shortly after that bout I bought my first pair of glasses. But simultaneously I was learning a great deal by preparing for lectures on interpersonal, group, and mass communication. Admittedly I also learned that the actor in me also enjoyed performing before large audiences.

I made a close, personal friendship with a Professor Richard McNally who taught the courses in classical rhetoric. He was a scholar of Latin and Greek and was able to teach me a lot until his untimely death from abdominal cancer. Dr. Kathleen Kendall had been the Acting Chair of the new Department who worked hard to recruit us to SUNYA in 1971. Kendall is a scholar of political communication who spent some time in the office of Nelson Rockefeller, the Governor of New York. Elaine and I remain in a close relationship with Kathy Kendall as I write in 2021.

I enjoyed lecturing on materials dating over hundreds of years and their roles in history as well as our modern, revolutionary work. But coming up with new lectures while chairing the department was somewhat taxing. Here is one of my favorite purely academic stories. I was at home in our dream house, coming down with a cough while scheduled to give a lecture to several hundred students the next day. Elaine gave me some cough syrup and I went to sleep. Ah, to sleep, perchance to dream. The next morning after the alarm awakened us, Elaine said that during the night I woke up, sat up straight and in my lecture hall voice delivered a lecture on "The Theory of Subcutaneous Rhetoric." She said it all made so much sense that she regretted not having pencil and paper to take notes.

When I got to the lecture hall and looked out to those hundreds of faces, I said it was wrong to begin a lecture or speech with an apology, but the fact that I had a chest cold produced an interesting communicative feat. I told them that my wife had given me a shot of cough syrup to help me sleep. I continued by telling them I sat up and lectured on the "Theory of Subcutaneous Rhetoric." I said that I wished she had taken notes so I could learn from the theory. At that moment, a hand went up on one the front rows. I pointed at the young man.

"Could you give us the name of that cough syrup?" It was the biggest laugh of the semester. Those were good times. Elaine and I both loved our work. She was an ABD, "all but dissertation" done for her doctorate at The University of Iowa. The RCO faculty and Dean of Humanities agreed twice to give me another three- year renewal as Chair. Toward the end of the nine years, a senior Editor at Wadsworth Publishing Company by the name of Rebecca Hayden got word of the course where she was in Belmont, California. She came to Albany and sat in on the RCO 100 class and then took me out to a nice place for lunch in Albany.

She said she heard about the course from one of Wadsworth's sales agents who also sat in on it. Becky, as she asked me to call her, said it was unique and revolutionary, inviting me to sign a contract for a book covering all the topics in the course. She stressed that there were no other courses out there, that a book covering these topics could do more to transform and grow the field of Speech into the field of Communication. I agreed.

I wrote a book for her: *Communication as Action: An Introduction to Rhetoric and Communication* (1982). Becky went to work on finding photographs of busts of ancient Greeks and Romans, and visual illustrations of more modern forms of communication. She placed appropriate artwork at the beginning of each chapter. It amazed me with its artistic, historic yet modern nature.

The title of my book, using the word *Action*, draws on Kenneth Burke's remark that "things move, people act." They act in two senses of the word: they are decisive and play to their audiences. The book begins with Burke's Definition of Man, the last word of which I had changed to Human. Here is a list of chapters:

Part One: Foundations of Rhetoric and Communication 3

1. A Definition of Human 4
2. Rhetoric Old and New 26
3. Communication Concepts 56

Part Two: Micro-Communication Settings 82

4. Interpersonal Communication: Several Dyadic Approaches 82
5. Triadic Communication 118
6. Group Communication 134

Part Three: Macro-Communication Settings 161

7. Organizational Communication 162
8. Communication and Social Movements 200
9. Mass Communication 220

The book sold well, particularly so considering that it had to inspire colleagues at other universities to create a new course moving them and their students into a new field. I was proud of it and still am, in addition to being grateful to Becky Hayden. As I write the first draft of this chapter in the spring of 2021, I have a package at hand with two copies of the *Communication as Action* mailed to me by a former student living in New York. I am to autograph them and add the name of two students who took the course at SUNYA in the 1970s, before the textbook was published. Thanks to Jim and Claire for asking.

I asked Wadsworth to send a copy to Kenneth Burke. His Definition of Man was included and retitled for the first chapter, making it [Hu]man. His ideas are woven into other parts of the book as well. I got a letter in the mail from

> Kenneth Burke
> 154 Amity Road
> Andover, NJ07821
>
> Dear Colleague, Phillip Tompkins
> Felicitations indeed on your *Communication as Action* volume. That strikes me as a very useful book. And it looks to me as though students that go through that mill are in for an excellent course. I was glad to see, on p. 48, that you brought up the "third application of identification." But I xxx (sic) wish that in discussion, you would bring out the twist whereby a specialist whose work identifies him with a company engaged in the production and marketing of a socio-economically noxious commodity can use this principle of identification in reverse. The subject was discussed in various aspects on pp. xxx (sic) of my *Rhetoric of Motives*. This issue is summed up in last two sentences of second paragraph p. 31. Nothing is more "liberal" than the principle of specialist autonomy; yet the twists are such that xxx dismal policies can be justified in its name. (Incidentally, I had in mind the distinction of this sort that Maritain had made.)

These words of KB are the salutation and first two paragraphs of his letter about *Communication as Action*. He left out the "p" in my last name, renaming me "Tomkins," the exact same mistake Truman Capote made in the letter quoted in an earlier chapter. But I forgave KB for it because of his felicitations and praise for a beginner's book. His reference to my discussion of the third application of identification provoked me to see what I had written:

> The third application of identification is also the most powerful because it goes unnoticed. Burke's example is "the word 'we,' as when the statement that 'we' are at war includes under the same head soldiers who are getting killed and speculators who hope to make a killing in war stocks."

He wanted me to stress in discussions that "one's morality as a specialist cannot be allowed to do duty for one's morality as a citizen. Insofar as the two roles are at odds, a specialty at the service of sinister interests will itself become sinister." Hmm, would that also apply to his example of the shepherd who takes good care of his sheep, protecting them from wolves and other threats, even though he is identified with a program that takes the lambs to market.

It would also mean that the CEO or Chief Executive Officer of a prosperous corporation might create conditions of high identification from top to bottom. It is common knowledge that today corporations pay their executives a salary that is many times the rate of everyone else. Bonuses are also provided for them at what some have called "obscene" amounts. Is that fair for them to persuade everyone that "*we*, all of us are in this together?"

Communication as Action was a part of the academic revolution in which the field of Speech became the field of Communication while retaining classical and adopting modern rhetorical theory. It was fun to be part of it.

Emily Makes Her Entrance

Five years into our marriage Elaine gave birth to our daughter, Emily Tompkins, on May 6, 1976. Her mother was troubled by cysts while pregnant so our daughter had to be taken by Caesarean section so that the troubling cyst could also be removed. When the nurse brought her to me, I checked her quickly for the symptoms Todd had shown. She had none of them and showed no sign of the strain of working her way through the birth canal, so in my relief and excitement I solemnly pronounced her "pretty."

"Most people say beautiful, but I am moved by your choice of words," said the nurse holding her. She could not have realized that I was checking the babe for signs of birth defects before I could pronounce the beautiful word I chose.

I hustled back to find out how Elaine had come through the surgery and to tell her our daughter Emily was pretty and much more.

Parting the Iron Curtain: Soviets Study Rhetoric

Although I am not sure of the date, let's say it was 1977 because Elaine was again teaching, and Emily was in the care of a babysitter. I was informed that although it was said, perhaps inaccurately, to be contrary to federal law, ten students from the Soviet Union would be allowed to attend the State University of New York at Albany. Ten American students from our campus would attend the Moscow Institute of Arts. I was approached by administrative powers of the university and asked to teach one of the classes they would take. They wanted me to offer a course in public speaking, including both composition and delivery. I agreed to do so. All I could find out was that Governor Rockefeller and his brother had enough political influence and money to pull off this feat. Dr. Kendall recently told me that she did not think it was the Rockefellers who made the deal. At the time I thought the Governor and his brother could accomplish almost anything they desired to do.

It reminded me of the time in the 1960s when Soviet rocket scientists met near, but not on, the Marshall Space Flight Center for a kind of academic convention. It was against the law, I was told, but the two groups presented state-of-the-art papers on the hardware solutions made by both groups while trying to equal or surpass each other in the capacity of their rockets.

Now I was going to teach young American students in the same class with older, more-advanced-educationally Soviet students. I got strong advice from an intelligence agent from the U.S. government who visited me. One of the ten students would be a KGB agent, he said, one who would report on the behavior of the other nine students. I was sternly advised never to repeat what one Soviet student had said to me in privacy to another because it might get to the agent and be used against the former.

I prepared a syllabus for the class and our first meetings were quite formal. We began with self-introductory speeches. The Soviet students were obviously older, more educated, and sophisticated than the American students. They spoke several languages, learned as preparation to serve in embassies, their version of our State Department, and perhaps even delegates to the United Nations. I introduced rhetorical theory in a rather practical way in my lectures and required that they demonstrate the use of analogy, induction, and enthymemes in their speeches.

Elaine suggested we invite them to our place for dinner and entertainment. Our house sat on five acres with a large pond stocked with bluegills and bass; there were small gardens, and tall trees, evoking the word "dacha" from one of the Soviet students, amending it by saying it was much larger than the small country homes in the Russian part of the U.S.S.R. Elaine had turned to Emily's babysitter, a Russian orthodox immigrant named Olga for advice about snacks and other foods. Olga recommended a Jewish delicatessen in Albany where Elaine could get Russian caviar and other delicacies. We hit the liquor store for a couple of bottles of Stolichnaya vodka imported from the Soviet Union. As we talked about the social event in class, some of the American students volunteered to bring the others out to our home in their cars to our place in the foothills just outside Albany.

When the twenty students had arrived, the Soviets insisted on giving me and Elaine gifts from their country. They produced a couple of bottles of vodka that we opened immediately. I must have talked about my love of classical music in class because they gave me an LP recording of pianist Emil Gilels, whom I had heard play in the Hall of Music at Purdue and greatly admired. I opened it and put it on the turntable at a low volume. I brought out the bottle of Stolichnaya and they were all eyes; they knew about the brand but had never seen a bottle of it, much less tasted it. It was made for export, the Americans later decided. They asked to hold it, taking turns to rub a hand up and down the bottle. I opened it and they were in heaven, swallowing a shot and then reveling in the aftertaste.

We showed them to an elegant buffet Elaine had prepared and we spent the evening standing, drinking, talking, and eating. The Soviet students seemed more relaxed, less guarded, than we had seen them on campus. Our designated drivers got everyone back home safely and the party was a great success. The American students seemed a bit less intimidated by their older classmates after that, perhaps preparing for a subsequent scene in the classroom that should have been acted out for a much larger audience in both countries.

Oh, and the vodka bottles they gave us were not so smooth as the one holding the Stoly we served, and when empty we put them on the shelf to show friends their flaws and unintended bubbles in the glass itself.

Rotten with Perfection

The buildup to the most dramatic scene in our educational drama came after both groups had given several speeches. I allowed for time they could use discussing rhetorical theory, criticism, ways of improving their speeches, and any other relevant topic. They had seated themselves in two different groups and one of the American students asked for recognition. I called on him and he said this:

"Well, after these several speeches we have noticed a pattern in the topics and stances taken by the two groups. We have been talking about social and political problems in the United States and what we should do about them. In your speeches you never talked about problems in your country. It makes us think you must be from a perfect system. That is my question: Do you come from a system that is perfect?"

Nine Soviet heads turned to look at the tenth person. *Aha*, I thought, *now we know* which one is the KGB agent.

The tenth student paused for a slow moment, looking down at his notebook and his hands, then he faced the other group and said "Yes."

Thus, we see the inability *or unwillingness to replicate*. The two groups were given the exact same assignment: the Americans criticized their own system, making proposals they thought could make it better. The Soviets were either unable or unwilling to express problems in their system.

Recently I went online to see about the Rockefeller brothers and student exchange programs. It is still in business. Kenneth Burke was appointed to a commission established by the Rockefeller brothers to study the effect of illegal drugs. He told me the "Rockefeller name opened all of the doors," just as I believe it had in bringing Soviet students to my class and sending SUNY Albany students to the Soviet Union.

The Soviet students' claim of perfection relaxed things for the American students. They became less intimidated by their foreign classmates in speeches and class discussions. I knew a professor in the Chemistry Department who had worked with students in a research lab in the Soviet Union. After telling him how the Soviets had admitted their system was "rotten with perfection," and how the American students challenged them to verbalize that assumption, the Chemistry Professor said,

"Those Soviet students will never be the same after your class."

While reflecting on our conversation a thought came to me—*nor will the American students. They will have a deeper understanding of how open communication assumes the freedom of speech guaranteed by our constitution.*

Once again readers can see the power of *replication*: Having each of twenty students generate a speech with the same assignment showed that ten could look to their own political system for needed reforms, the other ten could not. History showed that because of this failure to achieve *open communication*, their system could not solve its problems and they were forced to give it up. I do not think they have completely achieved it in their new system. People who would express criticism of Mr. Putin must be much more reserved and careful than those in the USA who criticize the policies of President Joe Biden.

The undergraduate student mentioned above who did the interviewing for us, Michael Lampert, had two majors: Communication and Political Science. He got several undergraduate students added to the Faculty Senate, and then got Dr. Phillip K. Tompkins elected Chairman of the Senate. We thought we had seen the last of him when this bright young man who grew up in the Bronx was admitted to Harvard Law School.

We still miss SUNYA and our large dacha, but we had recruited faculty with the hope of gaining a doctoral program. The system gave us no support in that regard. I had served three three-year terms when I received a call to return to Purdue University. We felt great sadness in leaving our Dacha in the Helderburg Mountains and the contrasting joy of New York City and the Hudson River connecting the two. But contrary to predictions, we were moving back to the Big Ten.

Chapter Ten
The Challenger Accident And the Truth in Replication

We had been called back to Purdue, well, Elaine was invited for the first time. I would become the senior professor of organizational communication after W. Charles Redding's retirement. One day I got the news while walking across campus. A student gave those within earshot the news: "Challenger is down." It was Tuesday, January 28, 1986, when Challenger exploded during liftoff, at 11:38 a.m. Seven astronauts were lost, including the teacher-astronaut Christa McAuliffe. Millions of school children watched the explosion on television.

Later that year I was recruited by a Dean of Arts and Sciences at the University of Colorado at Boulder to come out west to rebuild a moribund Speech Department into a modern Communication Department by giving me thirteen academic lines on which to recruit a new faculty.

One of my former graduate students at Purdue, George Cheney, who came to CU as a faculty member studied the mass communication coverage and accounts of the "tragedy." That word *tragedy*, Cheney found, was used over and over. Quite naturally I encouraged him to turn to Kenneth Burke's brilliant treatise on communication: *Permanence and Change*, for the best understanding of the word. He quoted Burke as writing about the "close connection between tragedy and purpose. We might almost lay it down as a rule of thumb; where someone is straining to do something, look for evidence of the tragic mechanism" (195).

I did not have the urge to write about a NASA failure, so I kept much of my attention on the fire seminar I was teaching, inspired by a Father's Day gift from my son Terry, *Young Men and Fire*. I taught an undergraduate course using that well-written book by Norman Maclean. Start with the concrete example of a wildfire and introduce definitions, research findings and theory *only* when the students ask questions. Such as, "What was motivating these people?" Now the students are asking for theory and research to answer their questions. For a term project, the students picked a concrete, real world organization to study and analyze. It worked.

In an earlier chapter I recounted my correspondence with the Nobel Laureate in Economics, Herbert A. Simon. He chipped into the riches of the fire seminar by highly recommending a book about the open communication practices of the U.S., Forest Service: *The Forest Ranger: A Study in Administrative Behavior* by Herbert Kaufman. Graduate student papers by Connie Bullis, Greg Larson, and others added to the readings. Readers interested in this work should consult Chapter 5, "Fighting Fires with Smart Risks," in my 2015 book, *Managing Risk and Complexity through Open Communication and Teamwork*.

The fire seminar also worked for our new graduate students at CU. One of those CU students, Greg Larson, wound up on the faculty at the University of Montana, taking the fire seminar with him. But my concentration kept coming back to the Challenger accident. I decided to write an article or two for an academic journal. I read the Rogers Report—the short title for the *Report of the Presidential Commission on the Space Challenger Accident*, headed by former Secretary of State William P. Rogers. It became available in June 1986 while I was in Boulder. I wore it out. Then I got in touch with the Marshall Space Flight Center, requesting interviews with some top managers in the hierarchy.

In an article published in *Communication Monographs* in 1977, I had written that the big surprise of my NASA experience was that I did not find a neat and tidy distinction between *Science* and *Rhetoric*, between *Demonstration* and *Persuasion*. Aristotle had written about *topoi*, or lines of argument available to a persuasive speaker. I discovered that in rocket science and technology that the Master Topoi were three in number: Reliability, Time, and Cost. In difficult technical decisions, these topoi could create places to look for arguments. Reliability is that "my recommendation will work consistently." Time is "my recommendation will keep us on schedule." Cost is "my recommendation is cheaper and within the budget."

No Foul Compromises

Most interesting to me is that on the most difficult decisions, von Braun created what he called a Working Group, a team of differing specializations, who could compromise. About these compromises, von Braun told me that "we always need to avoid the *foul* compromise." It was in that time frame that I first heard the word "tradeoff," in which I say to you "I'll give you some time if you will give me some cost and reliability." Another rhetorical manifestation was the clash between organizational identification and laboratory or other subunit identification. The latter involved being so identified with the specialization of one's lab that he favored it over identification with the project-as-a-whole. Powerful forces of organizational rhetoric were at work.

A Trip to Huntsville

On January 9 and 10 of 1990, four years after the Challenger tragedy, I returned to Huntsville to interview 16 top managers. They opened up to me immediately—some remembering me from my earlier work, others having heard of it. They were harshly critical of two previous Directors who came after von Braun, Rocco Petrone and William Lucas, the latter having resigned after the Challenger disaster. They gave me highly disappointing answers to my questions. Only four of the 16 administrators could define Automatic Responsibility.

The powerful Monday Notes had been submitted to von Braun in typewritten, hard copy so that he could react with notes in the margin. Now, while I was visiting they were sent up the line via e-mail but did not come back with written comments by the Director. This lack of response made the new notes a mockery of the dynamic feedback available to all the contributors of the original notes. Many of the interviewees said the whole communication system had declined in openness and exactitude. One of the communication blunders they mentioned was during the teleconference the night before the launch. The Contractor for Challenger was Morton-Thiokol of Utah. Their representatives recommended against the launch because the weather was cooling at the Cape and they had never *tested* the O-Rings, giant washers on the booster, below 53 degrees Fahrenheit. There is that word in Italics again.

The NASA officials from the Marshall Center asked them to prove that it would not fly. The Contractor could not prove a negative, so they caved in. The NASA officials got the Contractor personnel to change their recommendations. Dr. Lucas, who was the Director of MSFC at that time, testified to the Rogers Commission that had he known the concerns of the Contractor's engineers, he would not have ordered the launch. In this decision we have at least two disastrous communication failures. Decision makers ordered the launch without knowing the opinion of the Contractor's engineers. The second is that the NASA managers reversed the all-important rhetorical principle of the *burden of proof.* I had the evidence I needed for an important journal article in the relatively new journal called *Communication Monographs.*

Just before that year's National Communication Association Convention, I got a phone call from a man named Claude Teweles. He said he had opened a publishing company and would like to have lunch with me at the NCA convention. I agreed. When we sat down to eat in the hotel restaurant Claude asked:

"What are you working on now, Phil?"

"Well, I recently took a trip to the Marshall Space Flight Center to do some interviews about the Challenger disaster. The answers I got support a hypothesis of 'organizational forgetting.' Some of the important communication practices that helped make Apollo so successful are no longer in effect."

"What are you going to do with it?" he asked.

"Well, I wrote two articles for *Communication Monographs* about discovering those brilliant communication practices at the Marshall Space Flight Center in 1977. I think that would be the place for the explanation of the Challenger accident."

"I've got a better idea. Why don't you write a book for me, for Roxbury Publishing Company? Put together what you have learned from Apollo and now from Challenger?"

"That is what I plan to do in the articles," I replied.

Then I thought, *hmm, organizational communication is a fairly- young field. I could build a framework in which I can include the lessons of the two case studies.*

"In an appendix," said Claude, "you could put some questions for student discussions, and I could market it as both a scholarly- and text-book."

That conversation took place in November. Claude drew up a contract for us to sign and I began to think about using a slightly different approach than I would have used in a journal article. I got excited about the project as the fall semester was coming to close. Elaine had received a small inheritance from the passing of her Aunt Corinne. She gave our daughter Emily $100 for an opal ring she loved and the same amount to me with which I bought a fountain pen and a huge pile of legal pads.

I put them to work at the dining table in our house in North Boulder writing a book I had been persuaded by the publisher to do. Dorothy Parker's quip about "I enjoy having written" implied she did not enjoy the act of writing itself. I have experienced enjoyment during the process of *writing itself*. I was eager to get at that pen and pad even when eating or sleeping. I finished it during the Christmas break. George Cheney dropped in on me and asked what I had been up to.

"Writing a book? I had no idea you were going to write a book," he said.

"Neither did I."

George and I kept close track of each other during those days.

I wrote until I finished the book with Aunt Corinne's pen. Two stories, one of success that helped explain the other, a failure. Then I began to rewrite it on my word processor. Writing is rewriting for me. When satisfied with it I sent the manuscript to Claude Teweles. He was pleased with it and decided to publish it without an Index, a mistake. He got five scholars in organizational communication and plucked some juicy blurbs from their reviews for the back of the book. My mind had shifted back to classes and other research projects when I got another call from Claude.

"I hate to say it, Phil, but my lawyer says I must have certain quotes 'fact-checked,' so you must get permission from the unidentified NASA officials at the Marshall Center you quote in the book."

"What?"

"Yes. I have marked all of the quotations and have a draft of the letter to send them."

I do not remember having cursed during the conversation, but I was damned mad. Here you go, I said to myself, persuading me to write it and then I when it is done, I have to fact-check it. But I did write to 13 of the 16 persons interviewed, asking them for permission to quote them in the book. Those who are curious about the process can check the notes on ages 157-8 of the book: *Organizational Communication Imperatives: Lessons of the Space Program*. Those notes turned out to be "a kind of *replication* of the study, with the happy consequence of turning up the same findings in 1992 as in 1990."

Replication once *again* satisfies legal experts as the means of establishing the "truth." Recall that the *Esquire* lawyers required their Research Editor to verify all quotations in my article, "In Cold Fact," before it could be published. The successful replication gives readers confidence of the authenticity of both documents.

The book came out in 1993. It addresses the reader as a first-person narrative, a form that bothered some academics and may still do so. There is the belief of some that scientific or objective research should be done in the third person. I disagree with that claim by concurring with Henry David Thoreau that it is always the first person speaking—whether we acknowledge it or not. That book and this book acknowledge it.

Looking at the preface 24 years later I am pleased that it mentions a literary theorist and critic, William Empson, who discusses the double plot; in my case they are both nonfiction one taking place in the 1960s and the other in the 1980s, a way of dramatizing the importance of leadership and organizational communication as well as peripheral but important social factors. Looking again I see that I tried a trick Kenneth Burke taught me. He said that you should always look at what is happening at the mathematical center of a work. He used the analogy of a tunnel. As you enter it on foot or in your car you are moving internally, but at some *word* you reach the maximum point of internality. From there on you are moving externally, out of the tunnel. The book has 213 pages excluding appendages. Divide that number and the mathematical center is 166 1/2.

Half-way down the 170th page is a heading: “Saturn V flies.” The Moon Rocket is ready. The book goes on to the plot of the tragedy in its second half.

Organizational Communication Imperatives was published in 1993. *I am done with NASA and outer space*, I thought, unaware that there would be a call for a triple plot in the future.

Chapter Eleven
Seeking a Second Opinion

Before tackling what experts have to say about second opinions I turned inwardly. For more than a quarter century my wife Elaine and I have been members of the Kaiser Permanente Medical System. We have the same general practitioner, Dr. Alan Lidsky. Did I ever get a second opinion? Nearly every time Dr. Lidsky has thought I had a problem he refers me to a specialist. But I do not think I have gone beyond the KP specialists for a second opinion. Maybe I have been missing something.

Ergo, I turned to my former student and friend, Michael Lampert. Mike was a student of mine in the early 1970s at the State University of New York at Albany. He ran the campus, getting me elected Chairperson of the Faculty Governance Body. He went on to Harvard Law school and a successful career with offices in New York and London. He has mastered the electronic web and seems to enjoy teaching his former professor how to reap the benefits. Having access electronically to the Harvard University Library, he came up with some academic sources, a couple of recommended books and academic journal articles about the topic. I was so delighted by one of the books I shall recommend it to readers by means of summarizing it, while also working to organize the findings of several large empirical studies.

AARP Medical Advice

When it was time to stop working on those sources to eat lunch, I took my place at our dining table and saw a copy of *The AARP Magazine*. Elaine left it for me to read. I browsed through it while eating alone and saw a reference to an article on pp. 24-25 with this intriguing title: "The Art of Getting a Good Second Opinion," by Kimberly Rae Miller. I breezed through it and began to succumb. *Hmm*, I thought, why not start with advice from popular writers and then see how much support for it there is in the academic literature. And lack of support. I checked the date on the magazine for a couple of reasons and found this: December 2019/January 2020, a recent publication.

Miller begins her article with hypothetical interactions with two doctors. The first is a man who enters the room with the results of your tests. He is looking grim. He says you will have to begin the treatments immediately, putting you into a state of shock: Just do as he says.

The second interaction begins this way: Your physician enters the room, and she is smiling. The test results are all negative. The symptoms do not seem to be problems. Come back in six months and we will see how you are doing then. You are relieved, but then it does not seem right that you have these symptoms.

Miller then provides this direct advice:

"In either situation your next move should be the same: Seek out a second opinion."

Author Miller then refers to a 2015 study of nearly 7,000 people who got a second opinion. It was found that approximately 37 percent went on to a change in treatment. There was also a change in diagnosis for 15 percent of the patients. The author asks, if the chances are one in three that your doctor's diagnosis might not be right, do you not owe it to yourself to get a second opinion? After reading the article I sent off an email to the magazine asking for a citation of the study.

"Getting a second opinion is good medical practice," is a statement attributed to R. Ruth Linden, president of the Tree of Life Health Advocates in San Francisco. Miller attributes another quotation to the same person: "Medical knowledge is always changing; newer treatments are always in the pipeline. Clinical trials and other kinds of investigational procedures or therapies might be available."

When should I seek one?

This is the first heading of the article. The general answer is provided by quoting Sue Varma: whenever you get a first diagnosis "with serious implications." Examples include "being prescribed medication that has serious side effects; surgery; a life changing diagnosis; or costly procedures that aren't covered by your insurance." Another is when you have symptoms that are trivialized by a doctor or not judged to be serious: that is the time to seek a second opinion.

Am I putting my relationship with my current doctor at risk?

Under this heading Miller quotes Varma again as saying "Doctors ask their colleagues for curbside consults all the time." She says it is not uncommon for patients to fear what their physician might think about it, but a second opinion is becoming a routine part of medicine today. I did find, however, an empirical study showing that Japanese patients have a fear of offending their doctor; I will discuss that study below.

How do I make it happen?

Miller's first suggestion is to seek out others who have been given the same diagnosis and find out what they chose to do. "But it may be easier for you just to ask your physician for a referral. That will make it simpler to transfer records and test results to your new provider. If you are concerned that the first doctor's opinion might influence the second's, don't be." The answer to Why? is the claim that the second doctor will realize it is her or his job to make an independent evaluation.

Who pays for it?

I was starting to get impatient while waiting for affordability to come up for discussion. The first sentence on this question is: "Most insurance programs including Medicare, cover second opinions." But the "Golden Rule" according to Miller is to consult with your insurance provider in advance. It may be necessary to obtain approval prior to seeing the second doctor.

How do I prepare?

This one sounds as if it might be difficult for some patients. The recommendation is to gather all relevant records to pass along to your choice for a second opinion. Although it might be tempting to "start from scratch," duplication of tests might not be covered by your insurance plan. "Research your diagnosis, know what tests are customary, and prepare to ask questions."

What do I do if the two diagnoses are significantly different?

This final question is of considerable importance. The recommended answer is to seek a third and even a fourth medical opinion if necessary. Miller quotes Linden again to stress the point that patients do better going into treatment with confidence than without. From my perspective, replicating Capote came up with different results. The Research Editor at *Esquire*, in a second replication came up with the same results as I had. A strong third or fourth medical opinion might also come up with a strong agreement, one that would give doctor and patient confidence in the outcome.

A Second Set of Eyes

As soon as I had assimilated Miller's article my emeritus research associate Mike Lampert presented me with—and I will never understand how he found it—another popular article on the subject, but one with a different slant. The author is Michelle Andrews, her article is "Second Opinions are Often Sought, But Their Value isn't Clear." It was published in an online journal, *Shots: Health News from NPR*, May 26, 2015.

Andrews began the article with a photograph of actress Rita Wilson, smiling and waving a hand with the caption, "was diagnosed with breast cancer and underwent a double mastectomy, and told *People* magazine in April she expects to make a full recovery 'because I caught this early, have excellent doctors and because I got a second opinion.'"

The first set of eyes applied by writer Andrews leads to the observation that seeking second opinions seemed to be coming into vogue during that period five years ago. Even the redundancy of a second opinion agreeing with the first can "provide clarity and peace of mind."

"A second set of eyes, however," may see that a second opinion may uncover data missed or misinterpreted in the first opinion. The writer then mentions a study "that reviewed existing published research found that up to 62 percent of second opinions resulted in major changes to diagnoses or recommended treatments." No dates, authors, journal titles of the studies were cited. Another undocumented study was then mentioned: it looked at nearly 6,800 second opinions provided by Best Doctors, a "second-opinion service available as an employee benefit at some companies." The results: more than 40 percent of second opinions brought about changes among diagnoses and treatments.

"But here's the rub: While it's clear that the second opinion can help individual patients make better medical decisions, there's little hard data showing that second opinions lead to better health results overall."

The problem of the second opinion is then developed as a lack of data about the results. Which is better, the first or second opinion? In the case of the actress Rita Wilson, after the biopsies of both breasts in the first procedure, the pathological analysis did not find cancer. A friend advised her to get a second opinion; that pathologic analysis found "invasive lobular carcinoma." A third opinion or replication confirmed the second pathological diagnosis. There is a rough analogy to the Capote-Tompkins trials. Capote first published *In Cold Blood* in *The New Yorker* magazine. That organization had a favorable reputation for telling the truth. The fact checkers who processed "In Cold Blood" must have found no problems. When Tompkins made a rather full replication, or second opinion, he found serious factual cancers. A third opinion produced by the fact checker at *Esquire* agreed completely with the second opinion, or first replication by Tompkins.

In preparation for her conclusion, Andrews adds that second opinions may be costly to the patient, discussing procedures that insurance companies might not fund. The final paragraph:

Of course, asking for a second opinion doesn't necessarily mean accepting the advice. In the Best Doctors survey, 94.7 percent of patients said they either agreed or strongly agreed that they were satisfied with their experience. But only 61.2 percent said they either agreed or strongly agreed that they would follow the recommendations that they received in the second opinion.

Research on Second Opinions

Lampert used his Harvard University Library card to check out articles and books. I have chosen to begin with a study that was conducted by a medical organization in which I have an important personal interest my readers should know about. The study was conducted by the MD Anderson Cancer Center, University of Texas, in Houston, Texas. My daughter Kari Tompkins Lockett has lived in Houston for many years and was once accepted by MD Anderson as a patient referred to them by her primary doctor.

Second Opinions in Cancer Cases

The title of the study is "Second Opinion Pathologic Review is a Patient Safety Mechanism." The authors are Lavinia R. Middleton, M.D., Thomas W. Feeley, M.D., Heidi W. Albright, MHA, Ron Walters, M.D., and Stewart H. Hamilton, M.D., hereafter referred to as "Middleton et al." The study was published by the journal of the *American Society of Clinical Oncology*, Volume 10, July 20, 2014.

The attention and need steps of the article are combined in the claim that there is a "crisis in health care and delivery originating from the increasing health costs and inconsistent quality-of-care measures." They wrote that we need to know more about cost and quality of second opinions in cancer cases. During the entire month of September in the year 2011, 2,718 patients who had an original diagnosis at a tertiary hospital were referred to MD Anderson for another diagnosis. There was an agreement between the two pathological decisions in 75% of the cases. "In 25% of cases there was a discrepancy between the original pathology report and the subspecialty final pathology report; 509 changes in diagnosis were minor discrepancies (18.7%) and in 6.2% of patients (169 reports), the change in diagnosis represented a major discrepancy that potentially affected patient care."

The conclusion drawn in this large study was that the "second review improved clinical outcomes by providing evidence-based treatment plans for their precise pathological diagnosis." There is an elaborate diagram about costs that seems to support the idea that improving, or correcting, diagnoses save money.

Here is the final paragraph of the article:

"We believe that second review by a subspecialty pathologist demonstrates the value of multi-disciplinary cancer care in a high- volume comprehensive cancer center. The second review improved clinical outcomes by providing patients with evidence-based treatment for their precise pathologic diagnoses. We also demonstrated the cost implications of this practice and compared them with the costs of treatments avoided. Applied nationally, this added step before cancer treatment could improve the quality of cancer care in the United States."

The MD Anderson Cancer Center clearly believes that certain kinds of second opinion can improve the quality and cost of cancer treatment. Now I can reveal my personal interest in that organization. In 2008, my daughter Kari Tompkins Lockett was diagnosed by her physician, Dr. Amy Wood, as having cancer and referred her to MD Anderson. There she received surgery on her melanoma and says that you can hardly see the scar today, more than a dozen years later.

External and Internal Motivation for Second Opinions

This is an unusual study that I must include because my wife's maiden name is Vanden Bout. Yes, that is a Dutch name of which she is proud, making a stop in Amsterdam on our first trip together to Europe. Let me give the study a full citation before discussing it:

W.A. Mellink, A.M. Dulmen, Th. Wigers, P.M. Spreeuwenberg, A. M. M. Eggermont, and J.M. Bensing, "Cancer Patients Seeking a Second Surgical Opinion: Results of a Study on Motives, Needs, and Expectations." Supported by a grant from the Dutch Cancer Center, *Journal of Classical Oncology*, Vol. 21, No. 8, April 15, 2003.

The authors tell us that "The basis of the second-opinion consultation is a thorough re-evaluation of the patient care, including revision of diagnostic material." The study was done at the Department of Surgical Center and Daniel den Hoed Cancer Center in Rotterdam. The English written by these Dutch researchers is a bit difficult to translate, but they seem to be saying that human, interpersonal communication is vitally important to the practice of medicine and its second opinion. How could an Emeritus Professor of Communication disagree with that social scientific diagnosis?

Crucial to their analysis is a distinction between internal and external motivation in their study of 212 consecutive patients seeking a second opinion at the Surgical

Oncology Outpatient Clinic. These SOOC patients were given a questionnaire to complete. The average age was 53, young for cancer second opinions they say. Women made up 82% of the total, 76% of them had breast cancer. A majority of all the patients (62%) had only "internal motives for a second opinion." External motivation was for the patient to receive more information from the first doctor, a need to engage more actively in the decision making. The researchers emphasize that it is "necessary to develop strategies to prevent unnecessary second-opinion seeking." I can agree with that statement but only up to a certain point. The need for more information about cancer, to participate in a more equal situation is ultimately desirable. How can doctors learn this if their patients do not gain enough equality in first opinion interactions?

Study of Second Opinion in Japan

Earlier in this chapter I referred to a study of second opinions in Japan, one with social scientific implications. Again, I have a personal and professional interest in this study as an Emeritus Professor of Communication. The issue that tugs at me is one we once called "communication apprehension," a later development of what was earlier called "stage fright," the fear of public speaking. There seems to be a fear on the part of some patients, a fear of offending their doctor by asking for a second opinion. I was not surprised therefore to find a study of second opinions by Japanese doctors because it is well known that their culture places high respect for older citizens and people in authority.

The title of this study is "Values and risks of second opinion in Japan's universal health system," by Sawako Okamoto, Kazuo Kawahara MD, Atsushi Okawa MD PhD and Yuiiro Tanaka MD PhD. The article was published in 2013 as a Blackwell publication, *Health Expectations*, 18, pp. 826-838.

The authors begin by a survey finding that second opinion (SO) is widely recognized in Japan, but it is not known how patients view and use SO. Ergo, they took a survey of 356 respondents at Tokyo Medical and Dental University Hospital. Of their responses, 67 had experienced SO at a SO clinic; 82 had acquired SO without any instructions; 216 had neither sought nor received an SO. Results I found striking were these: SO patients better understood their illness, treatment, options, individualized plans, and uncertainty in medicine.

"More than half," however, "of the respondents misunderstood SO as a way to change doctors or treatments." This study gave the Japanese medical profession great motivation to improve *health communication*. The U.S. should also emphasize this kind of communication, encouraging our citizens to understand better when and why a second opinion should be sought—and not as just a way of getting rid of a doctor they do not like dealing with.

Second Opinion (SO) and Breast Cancer

Here we have a study of importance to the women of the world. The study was published in The *Annals of Surgical Oncology* rather recently, in 2018. The authors are Denise Garcia MD, Laura S. Sprulli, MD, PhD, Abid Irshad, MD, Jennifer Wood, RN, BSN, CBDN, Denise Kopecs RN, BSN, CBCN and Nancy Klauberp-De More, MD, FACS, "The Value of a Second Opinion for Breast Cancer Patients Referred to a National Cancer Institute (NCI) with a Multidisciplinary Tumor Board (MTB)," *The Annals of Surgical Oncology*, 2018.

The value of a second opinion was tested retrospectively with 70 patients seeking a second opinion. It was found that 30 of them (42.8%) experienced a change in diagnosis as a result of the MTB review. "The study findings support the conclusion that the referral for a second opinion is beneficial and has a diagnostic impact for many patients." These findings do not come as a surprise but should give hope to women who have received a first opinion that is distressing and difficult to understand.

Seeking Long Distance SOs

The professor of communication in me saved the best empirical study for last, even though it is tiny in the number of patients to be studied. But it is not the diagnosis itself that is studied here, it is media to be used over distance for such work. The reader will see at once, from the names of the authors, that it is an Italian study written in English. Their names, not listed with degrees: Martina Vincenzo Ferrari, Michele Marconi, Roberta Piazza, Andre Del Corso, Danielle Adami, Quintilia Lucehesi, Valeria Pagni, Rafalla Berchialli. The title of their study is "A tele-ultrasonographic platform to collect specialist second opinion in less specialized hospitals." It appeared in *Updates in Surgery* (2018) 10: 407-417. *Springer* is listed as the publisher.

The article begins with a discussion of rural areas and small cities, of how they have difficulty attracting doctors with specialties to live among them. The expenses of having the patients travel to urban areas are so great that it inhibits, prevents them from being seen and heard by specialists as part of a second opinion. The article is complete with diagrams of a patient sitting in a chair with some gadget being held against her or his stomach. Other diagrams show how the sounds and sights are picked up and transmitted to an expert's office far away. Visual and auditory media of communication are employed to help the specialist make a long-distance diagnosis.

I believe the abstract of the article captures the success and promise of providing second opinions over long distances.

Abstract

In non-urban scenarios: rural areas or small cities there is often a limited access to specialistic healthcare due to the inherent challenge associated with recruitment, retention, and access to health professionals. Telemedicine is an economical and effective way to address the problem. In this research, we developed a framework for real-time communication during ultrasound examination that combines interaction via standard video conference protocol and basic AR functionalistic (commercial) and a custom-developed application. The tele-ultrasonographic platform has been installed in a rural hospital in the Tuscan Apennines and tested on 12 patients. The study explores the utility of the system from the local and remote clinician perspective. The results obtained provide valuable insights: the platform and the telemedicine paradigm can reduce the costs related to the necessity to move the critical patients where there is a need for a specialist second opinion. Moreover, the possibility of having an expert guiding and commenting on the fly the diagnostic examination has also a didactic power and thus allows the local less specialized clinicians to grow in competence over time.

The teaching Professor still in me is thrilled to hear about the expert guiding and commenting "on the fly" with "didactic power" over long distances, increasing the competence of the local physicians.

Qualifications about Second Medical Opinions

I must hasten to say that second medical opinions are not all Exact replications. A doctor may recommend a second opinion because the recommended doctor has access to medical equipment not available to the first physician. Or the second doctor may have knowledge of medical procedures, e.g., tests, unknown to the first doctor. Indeed, those may be the, or one of the incentives, for making the second appointment. Nonetheless, getting confirmation by means of an identical diagnosis is also an incentive. Let us place those cases into the second category, the Conceptual replication.

Chapter Twelve
Columbia

Oh, no, I thought, *not another Shuttle disaster.* But it was. On February 1, 2003, *Columbia* broke up, killing seven astronauts. I decided not to pursue the case: four "data points"—an expression researchers use for trips to the well in studying an organization—were enough. And yet I could not stop reading about it. In April I was invited to give a lecture via telephone about it to a class in organizational communication at Michigan State University. I read all the newspaper accounts—daughter Emily helping me secure them electronically. She also helped me get the Report of the *Columbia Accident Investigation Board (CAIB)*, plus an important article in the *Atlantic Monthly*. Still, I resisted. It was so sad, and a tragedy as all parties strained to soar to the Heavens and return to Earth safely.

"Phil," said Greg Desilet, a golf buddy and philosophic scholar of Communication, "you have got to do it. You are the only one who can do it." I resisted. Shortly after that conversation, as I was walking down the 16th Street Mall in Denver, I could see a half dozen divisions or chapter titles in my head. I also heard from the man who persuaded me to publish my first space book, Claude Teweles. He offered me his top royalty rate and I signed a contract with him and Roxbury. (His publishing company was later bought by the Oxford University Press.) So, I went to work composing the results of my fifth data point, or research endeavor, with NASA. The title: *Apollo, Challenger, Columbia: The Decline of the Space Program* by Phillip K. Tompkins, "with the Assistance of Emily V. Tompkins."

An early riser, I would down some juice as I went to work on my computer at home, my first book-length work since retirement from the University of Colorado in 1998. Born with amblyopia, my brain failed to process information from my right eye. It provided only a peripheral vision of things to the right of me. I would wake up early, at times before dawn and get to work on the book. In the middle of the afternoon the one working eye in the writer's head tired and the need for communication via the ineluctable modality of the audible became keen. Elaine had retired from teaching at CU, and was working at our new church, Trinity United Methodist Church in downtown Denver, so I had to go out to talk to another human. I started finding my favorite bars within walking distance of our loft in downtown Denver: The Broker, Sam's No. 3, and others. I met a neighbor, a classical musical conductor during this routine who was something of a wit. He said we were threatening to become "bar flies." Back to the computer the next morning, sometimes as early as 3:30 in the morning.

Reception to *Apollo, Challenger, Columbia*

It was published in 2005 and rather than summarize a book available to the reader, I shall instead summarize the reception to this triple-plot drama. An early response came from a few miles north of Denver, from the Ball Aerospace Company in Boulder, Colorado. It was written by Dr. Stein Cass, an aeronautical engineer at Ball who had just finished my book. He was particularly interested in "how culture change and risk seem to be intertwined, especially for the change in risk perception on the Shuttle program." His reference was to a change of leadership at the top of NASA after Apollo. The new Administrator wanted to save money, so he proposed the goal and decision premises captured in this phrase: "Faster, Better, Cheaper," clearly differing from previous NASA decision premises. A culture battle took place at Bell Aerospace that Greg Larson studied for his dissertation, referring to Ball as JAR. The engineers hearing these new premises banded together to resist them, to maintain their high standards. I joined Larson in a paper that won an award and was published in *Communication Monographs* in 2005 under the title "Ambivalence and Resistance: A Study of Management in a Concertive Control System."

Dr. Cass thought they had reached the limit of the mathematical approach to risk and after reading my book he thought the communication approach could help. He invited me up to Boulder for lunch and began an intensive seminar-directed study of the mathematical approach:

$$RF=L*I$$

Risk Factor equals Likelihood times Impact

I read the history of mathematics and was amazed that the foundation, Euclid's *Elements*, had no numbers or equations. It had funny little geometric diagrams and words, verbal arguments about them. He made such tight arguments—avoiding any logical fallacies—that some readers could see that equations were possible. Digging further, I learned that Euclid was either a student of Aristotle's or had been taught by one of Aristotle's students. He therefore would have been well grounded in Rhetoric and Logic, thus enabled to make the case for Geometry.

Dr. Cass invited me to give a paper for the International Conference of Systems Engineers in Las Vegas on August 18, 2005. The title came to me after my crash course in math: "Communication as the Geometry of Human Organization: A Rhetorical

Analysis of Risk." It was fun to write. Here is a quotation: "The apex of the triangle, of course, represents the central authority. The sloping lines represent the former lines of communication and Fayol's definition of managerial functions such as commanding, coordinating, and controlling: these lines of communication *constitute* the geometric forms. The scalar chain of communication is that line of superiors and subordinates—many playing both roles—stretching from the apex, centralized command, to those at the base of the triangle, the workers who execute the commands." I turned Euclid's geometric designs into patterns of communication, working Einstein's Relativity Theory and Witten's String Theory into the discussion.

It was exciting but I was unable to make it to the Systems Engineering Convention to deliver the paper. Dr. Cass kindly delivered the paper for me and said it went well. I delivered it myself at an international convention NASA organized in 2005 at the Ronald Reagan Complex in Washington, D.C. Good friends Kathleen Kendall and Mike Lampert, as well as the other Dr. Tompkins, were in the audience.

Embry-Riddle Aeronautical University

It was exciting when I was invited to Embry-Riddle Aeronautical University in Florida. I had put my email address in *Apollo, Challenger, Columbia* and soon I heard from a young professor, Dr. Joanne Detore-Nakamura, at ERAU. She had read the book and was going to use it in a class. Could I visit her class and give a campus-wide lecture about the book with expenses plus a generous honorarium?

"Of course," and we visited Daytona Beach in January 2006, a nice contrast to Denver's ski weather. Her students were well into the book and full of questions and comments. I distinctly remember one large young man who raved about the Monday Notes. The lecture set an attendance record at the Miller Center Auditorium, with workers bringing in folding chairs for the overflow crowd. They had prepared wonderfully appropriate visual aids for the huge screen behind me, shots of von Braun, other NASA personnel, and of course the Saturn V launch.

"I want to begin by thanking Dr. Detore-Nakamura for making arrangements," adding "I'm still wondering how she got NASA to launch the Pluto Probe today so I could watch it from campus." It was high drama for this Emeritus Org-com Prof to be speaking to this special audience about the Space Program. All the students wanted to be pilots, astronauts, to be cast in some role in the aerospace drama. My speech was published in *Vital Speeches of the Day* for February 15, 2006.

NASA invited me back to present at their International Conference the next year, 2006, so I presented a "Lessons Learned" paper from the Triple Plot book about Apollo, Challenger, and Columbia—lessons I collected from professors who taught the book in classes, e.g., Greg Larson of the University of Montana, Joanne Detore-Nakamura and others.

ACC has continued to stimulate responses that amazed me. In 2017, twelve years after its publication, the book was read by eight students at the University of South Dakota taught by Professor Nicole Ackman, in Advanced Organizational Communication, SPCM 512. On March 6, 2017, classes were closed to open IDEAFEST on campus; students were encouraged to present ideas they had learned in class via posters. Eight ideas from *ACC* were presented by the students, one of them an enlargement of the organization chart representing NASA-MSFC of 1967, with parts highlighted to show the boxes of participants in the Monday Notes. This poster was prepared by Karol Eggers, who later mailed me the enlarged 40" by 60" version of the poster.

Eggers later sent me a letter congratulating me on being a "prophet." She said that Chapter Eight of *ACC* predicted the Great Recession of 2008. Here is what she wrote on April 14, 2017, at 8:10 p.m.

"Phil, I finished reading your book today. I'd say that I enjoyed it immensely, but you spent a great deal of time discussing undeniable truths about corporate culture that were hard to hear. You're correct on so many levels. I had to smile a little bit, knowing that you were making some pretty prophetic statements, considering that the book was written prior to the Great Recession.

Karol"

I had almost forgotten about that chapter: "The Challenger Syndrome and the Decline of American Organizational Institutions: 'Speaking Truth to Power." Adding it made the book a Quadra-Plot Drama—the success of Apollo, the failure of Challenger, the failure of Columbia, the failure of American businesses. I had been doing the research without thinking of an outlet when Omar Swartz, a friend and colleague at the University of Colorado Denver, invited me to deliver it as a keynote address at the Rocky Mountain Communication Association in 2003. It was well received.

Eggers's claim made me look at Chapter Eight again. I was concerned to show that it was not just NASA—a government bureaucracy—that was failing by faulty communication, by forgetting what we had learned during Apollo. No, a large section of American businesses had been exposed by some A-Plus journalistic research.

> On Thursday, January 9, 2003, seven days before the launch of the shuttle Columbia, the Public Broadcast System performed a great public service by presenting a Frontline show called "A Dangerous Business."

I turned on the television set in time to see much of it and knew immediately it was a story relevant to the thesis of a keynote I was to give nine days later, January 18, 2003. The next day I got a transcript of the program and learned that PBS, the *New York Times,* and the Canadian Broadcast Company had jointly investigated one of the most dangerous companies in America, the McWane Corporation, founded in Birmingham, Alabama in the 1920s. The company made sewer pipes in ten states and Canada. Here is a quotation from my summary:

> Until the journalistic investigation no outsiders knew of all the company's violations, which had been collected in various government offices around the country—there is no central file of their violations. McWane has received notice of more than 450 safety violations since 1995; respirators aren't provided to workers; machines lack safety guards; employees are inexperienced and untrained; flammable liquids are mishandled; forklifts don't have brakes. Nine workers have been killed in McWane's since 1995; at least three of these accidents were caused by deliberate violations of Federal safety standards, and safety lapses account for at least five other deaths (p. 205).

I am surprised by the degree of reserve in my discourse about these villains discovered in this tragic drama. Nine workers killed in a ten- year period! The cause: Disciplined management communication practices. The Safety Director in a McWane plant said he did not have the authority to shut down the production line in the name of safety.

PBS reported a naturally occurring experiment, a rare and invaluable happening. It also adds evidence to the pragmatic-truth-providing power of *replication*, whether natural or designed. There is another foundry in Birmingham, an older company with a safe workplace and environmental record. The firm is consistently rated by *Fortune* magazine as one of the best employers in the U.S. Its name is American Cast Iron Pipe Company, or ACIPCO.

PBS interviewed ACIPCO's CEO, Van Richey, on camera about the firm's culture and specifically whether workers and other employees could shut down the production lines for safety. The answer was that safety is number one, taking precedence over production. The founder of the company, John Eagan, left the organization to the employees and said the highest value of it would be the Golden Rule. The President of ACIPCO at the time was named J.R. McWane; he quit when the Golden Rule was made the basic decision premise and founded his own, yes, foundry, based on Disciplined Management and Communication Practices. Thus, the villain in this tragedy emerged as the devil, the opponent of the Golden Rule.

Chapter Eight moves on to cite some prominent U.S. business firms that were accused or convicted of fraud, mainly manifested in their communication practices. The companies included Enron, Lehman Brothers, Arthur Andersen, InClone, Merrill Lynch, Adelphia, Rite Aid, Worldcom, and Tyco. I quoted the "sage of Wall Street," Arthur Levitt, as saying that all of this presented a "systemic problem" caused by an "erosion of ethical values on the part of American business." I also translated the unethical practices into 11 transgressions of ethical organizational communication:

> (1) lying; (2) encouraging others to lie; (3) power plays that seem to be similar to political bribes; (4) failure to listen to subordinates; (5) plausible deniability; (6) ignoranti affectatas; (7) failure to reveal conflicts of interest; (8) the fear of speaking the truth to power; (9) asymmetry of information and the absence of transparency demanded by capitalism; (10) the suppression of "voice," the freedom of speech and assembly; and (11) the absence of feedback loops to maintain control, hence the absence of organization.

One needs translation: number six is pretending ignorance of misdeeds. It was first expressed to explain the Roman Catholic Church's reaction to reports of their priests having sexually molested children. I think it should be applied to organizational settings in general.

In re-reading Chapter Eight of *ACC* I did not find an explicit prediction that the Great Recession would crash upon us three years later. But I did find such widespread forms of lying that could not lead us to better times. I sounded the alarm, tried to speak the truth to power, and asked educators to help reverse the process by their teaching and criticism. I do thank Karol Eggers for claiming my alarms as a prediction and allowing me to say that if these practices are condoned again at large, we can expect the worst.

The Eighth Chapter of ACC did not consider the Replication Theory of the Truth, or RTT. Unlike the other three studies of NASA-MSFC I did, the two Apollo studies plus the *Challenger*, the study of *Columbia* was based on documents. Nonetheless it was a Conceptual Replication in the sense that I was looking at the same major variables of Communication as I had during the earlier studies. The findings were almost the same as with Challenger—the Organizational Forgetting of von Braun's almost magical practices of Open Communication.

There is another conclusion that is based on Replicative evidence. In 1968 during my second stint as Summer Faculty Consultant, I was supposed to ask my interviewees at the Marshall Center about their views of what kind of project they wanted to tackle after Apollo, the Post-Apollo period we called it. I reported back to von Braun that some of the people I interviewed wanted to tackle the Space Shuttle. He shook his head and told me "we should never put human beings on a rocket powered by solid fuel."

"Why?"

"Because we cannot test them or turn them off."

Testing, of course, was the second most important of von Braun's method of finding the truth in the R&D of the Saturn V, the vehicle of the Apollo Project. The first, of course, was communication, the process that gave him the results of tests by the Monday Notes, including at least several reports from different specializations, or Disciplinary Replication by redundant reports. This chapter allows us to see how two variablles worked together as in the title of the book: Replication and Open Communication.

Chapter Thirteen
Non-Replication in Psychology

During my years of teaching in the university, I told my students at every level, from freshmen to advanced doctoral students about the Chemistry experiments and to balance that truth I told them about "In Cold Fact" vs. *In Cold Blood*. In the middle of those two I would often talk about organizational communication during the Apollo Project. Most students respected those findings. One former student, Dr. David Noller, remembered so well that he made this chapter possible.

David's record of grades and test scores were so high when he applied for our graduate program in Communication at the University of Colorado at Boulder that he received the Chancellor's Fellowship. After he finished his doctorate, he took a job for a short period at SUNY Albany. He then worked his way to Los Angeles, California where he engaged in consulting work while trying to break into writing screenplays.

Remembering the replication lessons, he began to email articles to me about the use of such studies in the Academic field of Psychology. He sent me an article about a Psychology Professor made famous by her dissertation research. She developed an interesting theory to explain the findings so well that she became a celebrity, lecturing far and wide about her theory and experiment. As I recall, her income soared with her celebrity status. Then, someone had the nerve, the audacity, the ability to replicate her experiment. It failed, and the career as celebrity came to an end and so did her academic tenure.

I had written an earlier draft of this chapter that I somehow managed to lose. I found the article on which my profile was based but decided not to summarize it again using her name. That human being has suffered enough. Noller and other former students and friends have sent me many other articles about replications in Psychology. Another friend came up with a different gift for me. When I retired and we moved to downtown Denver from our house near the University of Colorado at Boulder, I lost face to face communication with academic colleagues. A member of the faculty and administration at the University of Colorado Denver welcomed me. He showed me the library at UCD I could use within walking distance of our loft. He invited me to give lectures to classes and other audiences. Dr. Omar Swartz has done many, many other favors for me as an Associate Professor and administrator for Legal Studies and Social Sciences at UCD.

I asked him for help and overnight he found and sent to me via the internet a full textbook: *Fundamentals of Social Psychology*, edited by the two authors of a chapter I had found myself: "The Replication Crisis in Psychology." The editors and authors are listed as Edward Diemer and Robert Diswas-Diemer. The book was published in 2018 by DEF Publisher of Champaign, Illinois. Replication is no doubt best known to American readers about the academic world, so for this chapter I thought let's give the readers a textbook analysis.

They begin with the conclusion that the science of Psychology is facing a profound crisis of their own making. The problem was, and apparently still is, the mounting number of formerly foundational experiments that have not been successfully replicated. They then take a close look at replication, dividing it into two broad categories: EXACT versus CONCEPTUAL, that I typographically changed to Exact and Conceptual earlier in this book. The Exact is illustrated by the Chemistry case I introduced earlier from my first faculty meeting. The Conceptual method occurs when "a scientist tries to confirm the previous findings using a different set of methods that test the same idea. The same hypothesis is tested, but by using a different method and measures (p. 7)." The reader now understands my source for the two types that I introduced earlier in this book. They are, as always, talking about scientists, but I think the Conceptual Method can also be used by the lay person as in my Literary-Rhetorical Method for "In Cold Fact."

The Diemer chapter moves on to a huge study published in the respected journal *Science*. They say it is an enormously large problem when only 37% of the articles published in four top scientific journals in Psychology were successfully replicated. They mentioned the "defensive" attitude of some psychologists whose work has been identified as a loser. Some professors, as indicated above in my opening of this chapter, have lost their job because of a failed replication of a study that had given them rise to prominence.

Why do replications fail? Three reasons are given: 1) researchers are "unskilled" or "unsophisticated;" 2) data are "falsified" or "faked;" 3) small sample sizes that may not be representative of the population from which they were drawn and about which they generalize.

Some readers may be disappointed by the solutions they advocate: Six principles of Open Science: Openness in Data, Sources, Access, Methodology, Educational Resources. I find it hard to criticize Open Communication after using the words in a book title published in 2015 and used as one of two major factors that help establish truth.

The authors say there are some reasons that support the interpretation of innocence. A small sample size of humans in an experiment could be statistically significant by accidentally skewed numbers, the lack of a representative sample of the population. The large samples give greater chance of representativeness. Here is a striking claim about the milieu of experimental psychologists: "The reward structure in academia has served to dissuade replications" (p. 13). Fame and rewards go to the published study that attracts media attention and makes the author a celebrity. Single studies are rarely useful. In fact, the authors' conclusions seem to suggest that single studies should not be published in journals.

I would agree with that in an experimental field such as Psychology, but in other less "scientific" fields that might not always be possible. I should like to raise another issue for Exact vs. Conceptual studies: Who should do the replication to get the best results? For an original study sent to be reviewed for publication, I suggest a novel method: The academics doing Study 1 might enlist other researchers to replicate it, making Study 2. The researchers of the original Study 1 would explain the theory from which the hypotheses were drawn and details of the first experiment. The second study would be submitted either as an appendix or as a separate article.

No matter how the future of psychological studies will be conducted and published, more attention should be paid to the competence and goals of the replication practitioners. I think again of the ICB-ICF controversy. We could not have trusted Capote to do his own replication, but the fact-checkers at *The New Yorker* where it was first published, certainly *failed*. As the replicator in the Clutter Case, I was an academic who learned to seek the truth, had no motives to make the replication succeed or fail. Once I had the results, I knew I had to publish them. They constituted a Conceptual Replication because I did not have laboratory or experimental control over the conditions, but I did have access to the written confession and the *literal* transcript of the trial, and interviews with surviving principals.

Recall that the editors at *Esquire* also conducted a Conceptual Replication when the Research Editor called all my identified sources of quotes and asked them if I had interviewed them, and if the quotations attributed to them were correct. *Esquire*'s motives were to get to the truth, not to attack Capote for some wrong he committed. They feared lawsuits brought by Capote's lawyers, and let their lawyers do the only substantive editing of my article.

I hope the science of Psychology does find a solution to its massive problems of replication failures. Their solutions may be useful to the other social sciences and who knows, perhaps the humanities, social sciences, and even lab sciences as well.

Chapter Fourteen
Risk, Art, and PTDL

The year was 2015, the one that saw me receive a great honor in addition to a new book by Phillip K. Tompkins. It started when I looked at my computer screen and saw Dr. Marifran Mattson reach out to Purdue alumni via the internet. And we began a conversation via email. I came to learn about her message-by-message as a friendly, admirable, courageous scholar-administrator as the Head of the Lamb School of Communication in the School of Liberal Arts at Purdue University. She does her job without complaint, despite having lost a leg when her motorcycle was hit by a huge truck. When the pain is too much, she cannot wear her artificial leg and must rely on crutches.

I told her that I was writing a book on managing risk and was thinking of submitting a proposal to the Purdue University Press. In my second life at Purdue, I served as Associate Dean of Liberal Arts and was a member of the Editorial Board of PUP, one of the best jobs I ever had in academia. We saw the book proposals, voted on them and got free copies of new PUP books. I loved telling others that the best-selling book ever published by PUP was *Hoosier Home Remedies*! Marifran said she would give me the name and address of the then-current Director of PUP, but we agreed that it would be unethical for her to try to assist me in any way after that.

As indicated earlier, I enjoy writing, but doing it for a deadline can be painful, particularly when the right way to write it does not come easily. But when I wake up in the morning at 3:30 a.m. with the words flowing, it is difficult not to pick up the pen or begin fingering the keyboard. I read most of what Hemingway wrote and most of what was written about him. I read about his habits when he was living in Havana and I learned a key lesson.

Hemingway would get up in the morning and write for two hours, standing up as I recall. But he always quit knowing what the next paragraph would be. The next day he went to work on his typewriter pounding out that paragraph. And sure enough, as Burke said, one act motivates another act. The first paragraph motivated the second paragraph and so on until another paragraph was saved for the next morning. I used that principle and rarely if ever experienced writer's block. (I watched with interest the documentary aired on PBS in the spring of 2021 about

Hemingway. There were images of the author standing at his typewriter and quotes of him delighting in knowing what he was going to write the next morning.)

I chose a title: *Managing Risk through Open Communication and Teamwork.* Chapters about the great success of Apollo and the failures of Challenger and Columbia were followed by chapters about medicine—including surgery; fighting wildfires; the "at risk" and "risky" homeless people I had been serving at the shelter where I volunteered; the Aviation Safety Reporting System; and a concluding chapter.

Before I had written all of them, I sent several chapters plus a proposal to the Director of the Purdue University Press, Charles Watkinson. I found him to be an astute reader with high standards. He sent it out to an anonymous reviewer who recommended it for publication even though he or she had reservations about the appearance of the first-person pronouns. The production editor, Kelley Kimm, was a dream come true. Feeding me questions and suggestions that were helpful, this intelligent reader-editor made it a better book.

The book was scheduled for publication in June of 2015, so I scheduled a signing at the Tattered Cover Bookstore, one of the largest independent companies of its kind in the country for years and a few blocks away on our main artery in Denver, the 16th Street Mall. We were all surprised when 55 or so people showed up for the signing. After talking about the contents of the volume, I signed copies of it. We sold enough to be on the best seller list of the *Denver Post* for a couple of weeks. Four men who seemed to know each other bought seven copies of the book for me to sign.

"How can we get in touch with you?" a large man asked.

"I put my email address in the book," I said, an answer that one of them later said, with a laugh, made him read the whole book. It worked. Soon I got an email message from Ryan Fields-Spack, a fire chief in Aurora, Colorado, the third largest city in Colorado. He proposed that we meet for coffee at a Starbucks near our loft in downtown Denver. He said "I am excited to meet with you because we are so similar in our research interests! I recently graduated from the Naval Post Graduate School in Monterey with a Master's in Security Studies (Homeland Security and Defense). The primary focus of my thesis was improving the collaborative capacity of police and fire agencies on active-shooter type incidents. The crux of this thesis stems from the Aviation Checklist, CRM and of course, Atul Gawande's 'Checklist Manifesto'!"

Wow, we even had the same sources, I thought, remembering the coverage I gave in the book to Dr. Gawande's findings and recommendations. We had a good meeting over a cup of coffee, and I agreed to meet with Ryan and two other commanders at the same Starbucks near our loft. We had all shaken hands at the Tattered Cover signing, but we met again. Mike West, Commander of the South Metro Fire Rescue Authority, and Commander Mike Stanley from the Aurora Fire Department. More common ground was explored by us and we made appointments to continue our conversation. Mike Stanley, for example, invited me to his station for a tour and then a ride in a Commander's Fire Engine. He got a call while driving us to report to a fire and the excitement grew inside me, that "high" that firefighters get in anticipation of an incident. I was both disappointed and relieved when our call was cancelled.

Elaine and I met with Ryan to help him with the composition and delivery of the paper he had written about his thesis. He had been invited to deliver it to a national conference on Homeland Security in 2015. We read his thesis and paper, reserved the Conference Room in our building to listen as professors of Communication to his rehearsal. We knew that he was a bright guy from conversation, the thesis, and paper; his presentation was effective also. We made suggestions to improve it, the most important one of which was a paragraph about the problems between police and firefighters when they arrive at shooter-type-incidents. He had mentioned it in his oral presentation, but it was important to expand it in the papers.

We wished Ryan well when he left for the Ninth Annual Homeland Security and Defense Education Summit in September 2015, held at the Naval Postgraduate School Center for Homeland Defense and Security. He later said it went well. In his presentation he did stress what we had recommended: "After action reports from shootings at Virginia Tech, Navy Yard, Aurora, etc., all speak to the need to improve collaboration among all first response agencies." I had learned from the infamous Aurora Theatre Shooting document Ryan shared with me that police and fire departments were criticized for not cooperating in the immediate aftermath.

He was proposing a three-step program of: (1) Making introductions such as shaking hands and exchanging names when police, fire, and medical personnel arrive on a dangerous scene. (2) Teamwork among the different organizations facing disastrous events, some of which might be sponsored by terrorist groups. (3) An adaptation of CRM, Crew Resource Management, or pre-flight briefings used by airplane flight crews. These were specific solutions to problems I did not understand completely, but he was strongly recommending Open Communication.

Mike Stanley and I continued an intense conversation. He talked to me openly about political problems in Aurora and answered my questions about firefighting. Elaine and I became good friends with Mike and his wife Sandy, aka "Lucky." Mike explained more about the problems in communication between fire and police forces. In Denver, the medical responders are housed and work with the Fire Departments as first responders. There are several causes of problems between and among them.

For example, the police get to the scene—yes, as in drama—before the fire engines. They pull up in front to park as close to the building being threatened as they can, sometimes double parking. This creates a serious problem when the fire engine pulls up and needs to get as close as it can because of the limits of the length of its hoses. Once they are all there together the police have a more militaristic command structure than the fire/medical personnel. The boss barks out orders to be obeyed.

Mike asked me to lecture to classes he taught for the fire department in Aurora and for Metro State University, across the Cherry Creek from our loft in downtown Denver. In one class I followed one of his fire-fighting colleagues who talked about a case in which they had a plan for entering a building on fire. Once inside, the conditions were much worse than expected. He and others had to make decisions on the spot, the first of which was to abandon the original plan. Informal communication and flexibility were needed.

As I write this passage it dawns on me that the next conversation I have with Mike or Ryan I must ask if they read the section of my *Managing Risk* book dealing with von Braun's practice of *penetration*. Recall that von Braun was called before Congress to testify about why his contractors did such a better job for the Marshall Space Flight Center than they did for other government agencies.

"Penetration" was his one-word answer. He saw to it that his personnel infiltrated contractor organizations, got to know their workers. They reported back to von Braun's organization what they had learned; we came to know better what was going on than the contractors' managers did. Would that work with horizontal organizations? Firefighters getting to know police personnel better between fires might help the interorganizational flow at the scene of a disaster.

The PTDL

After the signing in the Tattered Cover, I received an invitation to deliver the First Phil Tompkins Distinguished Lecture at Purdue University in October of 2015. I was floored to be offered the leading role in a drama of honor. I was informed of the honor by Dr. Marifran Mattson, the Head of the Lamb School of Communication; she said the faculty had voted to bestow the honor on me. The College of Liberal Arts and the university administration also approved it.

I accepted the role and learned that during the several days of our visit there would be a book launch and signing of *Managing Risk and Complexity through Open Communication and Teamwork*. There would also be meetings with archivists in the University Library about the donation of my papers to the university. We began to make plans. Daughter Emily and her husband Tofer Lewis would accompany us. They stayed in a motel, but I asked for Elaine and me to be housed in the hotel within the Memorial Union, yards away from Heavilon Hall, where I spent six years as a graduate student and an Assistant Professor.

I had first seen Marifran in a live video sent out to alumni. I caught her while still live and started a conversation. She was so graceful that I had no idea that she was an amputee. I learned of this while conversing via email with her. She was riding a motorcycle and collided with a semi-trailer.

"Do you mind if I mention your amputation?"

"No," she answered. "It is what made me strong."

I went to work on the PTDL, following Professor Mattson's suggestion that I direct my remarks to "graduate students old and new with suggestions about writing." *Hmm, what do they need to help them?* After the ritualistic introductory remarks, I quoted from that "learned poet," W. H. Auden's Phi Beta Kappa poem at a Harvard University graduation ceremony in 1946. What follows is my PTDL:

Text pf the First Phil Tompkins Distinguished Lecture

Thou shalt not sit

With statisticians nor commit

A Social Science.

After getting my Ph.D. degree here in 1962, Alan H. Monroe, the Head of our School of Speech, appointed me as an Assistant Professor. My first faculty meeting was of the entire university, held in the Hall of Music ("the World's Largest Auditorium," according to our PR department back then). The Dean of the Graduate School took the stage, called the meeting to order and said it was the "saddest day of my career." He then recognized the Head of the Chemistry Department.

The Head introduced a motion to rescind a Ph.D. degree granted by his department. A subsequent student could neither build upon nor *replicate* his findings. There was other evidence which persuaded us to vote unanimously to rescind the degree. [I could see members of the audience looking at each other and shaking their heads.] Do you remember that old saying, "There is one thing they can't take away from you?"

Three years later, Bruce Kendall, a professor here at Purdue and a mentor-friend for years, sat me down to read *In Cold Blood*, the sensational "non-fiction novel," about which the author, Truman Capote, had said "Every word is true." I doubted that claim, so I *replicated* his methods by travelling to the scene of the crime, four murders, and interviewed the same people Capote did, read the transcript of the trial and the confession of Perry Smith, one of the two cold-blooded killers of the four members of the respected Clutter family. An article in *Esquire* magazine, "In Cold Fact," earned me $600 and national fame. Yes, Purdue taught me what I call the practical, conceptual, and rhetorical test of truth: replication.

Next, I want to talk about how to read and write. Yes, graduate students need to know these skills—and young professors do as well. Let me share what I have learned about reading and writing. As a graduate here at Purdue I was buried in notes I had taken while studying for three graduate stat classes, two econ classes, two sociology courses, as well as my work in rhetoric and communication. In my classes I could rarely find the point I wanted to talk about because the notes were so voluminous.

I found a pamphlet about how to read for such purposes: Read the chapter or article closely, close the cover and write down an outline of the main points. Then open the book and compare your notes with the original. I quickly got the hang of it. Then I did not have to take notes, I could close my eyes and review the main points. In my classes I could speak from memory about the main points covered in the assigned readings. I learned in comm classes that I was taking the time to transfer those main points from the short-term memory to the long-term memory. Try it—it works. [I saw students furiously taking notes on what I was saying.]

I recently had lunch with two assistant professors in Denver. I asked them what advice they would give to graduate students about learning to write. One of them had worked with a Purdue grad who is a prolific writer, George Cheney. He quoted him as saying "Write as if someone will have to read it." Hemingway's rule: Always end a writing session knowing what the next paragraph would be. [In the fist of three episodes of "Hemmingway" shown on PBS in April of 2021, the author is quoted as saying he is happy because he has had a good day writing and knows what he will write the next morning.] You, the reader, must trust me on this next tip because I have never seen it in print, but a highly credible source told me about it. And it fits my experience.

The writing program at an eastern university divided their students into two groups for an experiment: the best and worst writers. They gave them a writing assignment and watched them go to work. The good writers were quick to abandon a sentence and start over, trying to let it flow well. The not-so-good writers kept at it, trying to repair the sentence, adding more and more clauses, unable to give up on a bad start.

"Thou shalt not commit a social science." Why did the poet write that line? Because he knew the reputation of social science writers for turning out prose that seeks to be so "scientific" there are no human beings conducting the studies or being used as subjects in them.

In writing your prospectus, follow Karl Weick's suggestion that you use future-perfect tense: "When I complete my project or thesis, *I will have done* the following." I asked my students to do it before setting out even on a term paper. Next tip: Never use the word "very." An eminent publisher, editor, and writer of the 20th century named William Allen White thought the word "very" was *very* much overused [very much laughter]. When White was tempted to use the word, he substituted the word "damn," or some other curse word that he would later have to remove.

Yes, the first PTDL gave me a feeling of one-ness, identification with, and gratitude to Purdue University for making such a big difference in my life. I had first studied communication there and was called back to talk about it.

Replication in the Art of Painting

If you look at the back of the *Managing Risk* book, you will find four block quotes about the book. I reproduce the first quote here:

> Essential insights from a career of world-class research! Tompkins's many years of distinguished scholarship culminates in a remarkable volume demonstrating the vital role organizational communication theory plays in solving our most pressing institutional problems. Spanning the full range of Tompkins's contributions, *Managing Risk and Complexity* delivers the knowledge today's managers and scholars must have to navigate twenty-first-century organizations.
>
> James R. Barker, Professor and Herbert S. Lamb Chair in Business Education, Rowe School of Business, Dalhousie University

I am grateful for this generous testimonial from one of my outstanding former students. One of those studies summarized in the beginning of the book is by James R. Barker. In addition to this connection, today I Googled the words "Concertive control," and up popped the name of Barker and his book: *The Discipline of Teamwork: Participation and Concertive Control,* by the same James R. Barker. Readers will remember that I have mentioned Concertive Control in this book as a theory I first articulated. Google says Professor Barker "developed" the theory. Try it for yourself. Barker studied with me for his M.A. degree at Purdue, went off to the Viet Nam War for his military service, then joined us as a doctoral student at the University of Colorado.

He did another noteworthy act by assigning *Managing Risk* to a Financier in Canada named Rick Ducommun. He liked the book and got in touch with me from his home in Cochrane, Alberta, Canada. He said he was going to drive to Pennsylvania with his dogs, get married and bring his bride and their dogs on a honeymoon to visit us in Denver. How could we resist? He and Laura were married on September 17, 2018. They arrived and found a motel on the outskirts of Denver where they could keep their dogs while visiting me and my wife Elaine.

They arrived in town on Friday morning while I was working as a volunteer at the St. Francis Center, a homeless shelter, so I gave the attractive bride and handsome groom a tour of the shelter. They were interested in our work and we moved on to lunch and our first meeting in the Tompkins loft in downtown Denver. He presented me with a framed 4" by 6" painting inspired by my book. I have reproduced it in this book because I was fascinated and charmed by it. Jim Barker must have seen it also because he advised me to look for the rocket blast in the small abstract painting. Rick and Laura took off to continue their honeymoon trip to their home in Canada.

Replication in the Visual Arts

Rick and I continued a lengthy email correspondence. During an exchange he learned of my interest in replication. He seems to have thought about it in relation to art. I kept encouraging him to send me more of his ideas. In his early observations he seemed to make some basic points. First, there is literal or exact replication in art. By that he meant first to establish that I had close if not exact copies of paintings by Winslow Homer, Georgia O'Keefe, and Pierre-Auguste Renoir that he had seen hanging in our loft. These were like photographs in the exact size, texture, and hues taken of the originals. That is the easy one. Then, Rick said that to establish a reputation by showing that she or he can paint in such a way that reflects or is similar to the dominant paradigm in visual art of that moment. He did not use the word "paradigm." I borrowed it from a powerful book by a philosopher, Thomas S. Kuhn, *The Structure of Scientific Revolutions* (1962). The book made a deep impression on me, showing that a science has a dominant paradigm, a kind of interpretive theoretical scheme for research. Then along comes someone with new findings that do not fit the existing Paradigm. So, someone must come up with a new Paradigm, a general theoretical framework that is consistent with a new finding and encourages a new kind of research studies. In fact, failure to replicate might encourage some to interpret the unexpected findings with a New Paradigm. Rick might not agree with my interpretation, but it is easier for me to discuss Art by means of a scientific analogy of Paradigm than any other.

Once the artist has established that he or she can paint in a style or school recognizable by the existing Paradigm, to become a great artist, the person must then establish a new style of painting, one that creates a New Paradigm.

This is my understanding of what Rick was teaching. Then his most inclusive expression of his ideas came in a long email dated October 31, 2020.

"The thought around the topic of replication in art, to me, is still that there is a paradox between originality (creativity) and constancy (validation). The first job of the critic is to find references to other works, then to challenge whether the subject's works are both new and replicable."

Rick thankfully introduced a great artist into the conversation known by most: "The artist is to create a concept, then demonstrate that said concept can be replicated. Had only one Van Gogh picture survived, then he would be destined to be traded at the price of his materials at best. That he expressed himself over and over again, he showed that he was never a one-piece wonder."

Rick might surprise some by clearly claiming that artists do some form of copying each other: "That very replication switches to formulae rather easily, especially given our wish to preserve so much visual data. The replication itself can be misused in politics through to advertising. Just because one can copy a visual expression, one isn't necessarily right, and certainly not creative."

He continued with a new, short paragraph: "Conversely, the lineup of people who crib other ideas, then claim ownership or originality approaches infinitely long."

"Creation and replication are a paradox."

Does this help, Phil?"

Yes, Rick, it does.

And so also does a paragraph he had sent on May 20, 2020:

"Hi Phil,

Okay, and here goes:

The paradox of visual art is taste and sophistication versus uniqueness and originality. Picasso had to demonstrate how he could manage artist materials in order to prove his sophistication to his instructors at first. Then he had to deviate in order to gain the attention he needed in order to have his artistic place. Whether the artist developed cubist notions of pictorial space and object restructuring – as Cezanne did—or whether he only replicated and rearranged long established artistic ideas isn't controversial anymore. He has come full circle, from plagiarist to sophisticate then original creative genius and now subject of unsophisticated replications.

Is this okay for you, Phil?

Rick"

I then asked Rick to explain how we first got together. He read my most recent book, *Managing Risk and Complexity through Open Communication and Teamwork*. As mentioned above, he was inspired to paint two small works and bring them to me in Denver while on his honeymoon with his bride Laura and their dogs. I asked him how the inspiration worked:

On February 3, 2021, Rick sent this reply:

"Hi Phil, and here goes.

To find oneself artistically is an ongoing struggle. We fight to find a fine balance between formalized repetition and boredom and the lack of controlled skills needed to create a work in whole. Phil's ideas and words helped me understand how to manage that grey zone. In return, I made several series of works that expressed the tension lying in the middle ground. I called the two pieces Managing Risk and Complexity Through Visual Communication."

This reminded me that Gregory Desilet warned me to keep replication and repetition apart. But while reading and seeing what Rick Ducommun is producing, I think he expresses the artistic counterpart of science.

National Institute of Standards and Technology

Mike Stanley and I became close friends, as were our families. He got an offer a couple of years later to become the Fire Chief of Oshkosh, Wisconsin. The job included coordinating six fire stations in Oshkosh. We kept in touch via email. Then I got the message in October 2020 that he had received an award. Below are the words in a clipping from a local paper in Oshkosh:

> On October 28th, Chief Mike Stanley of the City of Oshkosh Fire Department (OFD), received the Firefighter Hero Award from the National Fallen Fire Fighters Foundation (NFFF) and Maglite.

There was a photo of Mike being surprised by the announcement that he was named the national "Hero" of the year for his work in saving lives among homeless people and retired people in nursing homes.

Not long after receiving the award he needed to make a trip back to Denver and Aurora to see his daughters and conduct some business. He asked if we could meet in the Brooks Tower Conference Room wearing face masks. I got the key and met Mike in the lobby to take him, with mask, up to the third-floor Conference Room.

I was sure it was six feet across the table as we talked with each masked other, sharing news about family before getting into the business of firefighting. I complimented him on being named a Hero and he explained it a bit. He said he tried to keep up with research done by NIST. In addition, he said he knew how important my work at the homeless shelter was to me, so he looked carefully at the conditions of the shelter in Oshkosh. He made recommendations there and at the nursing home, suggestions about how to avoid falling, the number one cause of death by physical accidents among people aged 65 and older. He said that NIST was doing research that was also changing the way fire fighters fight fires.

I asked him about NIST and the research they do that is changing the way to fight fires.

"National Institute of Standards and Technology," he explained. He said that they bought abandoned houses and other buildings in which they conducted experiments with fires and how to fight them. I was interested so he promised to send me a link to NIST when he got back to Oshkosh. We touched elbows as we said goodbye.

Always reliable, Mike sent me a link to documents produced by NIST. I scanned them and learned that they did research in different parts of the country, including New Jersey and on Governors Island, just south of the southern tip of Manhattan. They said they tested the "conventional wisdom" of fire departments and reported their findings back to them. I wanted an example for this book, so I studied their experiments on different winds fanning blazes, but I did not completely understand more than the direction of attack is important in some kinds of fires. I did understand that fires in buildings consume all the oxygen and there is a strong sucking action when one opens a door or breaks a window.

After looking through the NIST documents from their website, I came to a place to ask them questions. So, I asked: "Do you use the principle of replication in your research?" I have not heard from them yet, but I did run across this promise to their readers. NIST said of their research in general that it is "capable of being substantially reproduced." I took that as meaning they considered being "reproduced" as having been replicated in order to be truthful. But then it could be they wanted to give the impression of replication. If any reader can either support or refute their claim, please send your message to Tompkinp@Colorado.Edu.

Oh, when Mike was leaving, I asked him if he used any of the NASA techniques of Open Communication.

"Automatic Responsibility," he said with a proud smile.

Chapter Fifteen
The Pandemic and Election of 2020

Smart Thermometers and Coronavirus

I had long admired Rachel Maddow of MSNBC. Brilliance may not be an exaggeration of her mental and communication capacities; over the years of watching her sixty-minute program from seven to eight p.m. here in Denver, I caught on to her method. To prepare for the evening lecture plus interview, she reads the most important newspapers in English relevant to the news of the day. And although she appears to speak extemporaneously from notes, her oral prose suggests a written text, one that could be read as a newspaper article itself. One night's show grabbed me so much that I had to ask Elaine for permission to watch nearly every night to keep up with the virus via Rachel's fluent reports during the crisis. One evening she gave credit to a New York *Times* journalist, calling him the best, most knowledgeable journalist writing about the coronavirus.

She produced on the screen the title of an article published earlier, on January 16, 2020: "'Smart Thermometers' Track Flu Season in Real Time," by Donald G. McNeil, Jr. She then gave us her oral summary with visual aids: A company named Kinsa Health, founded by the current CEO, Inder Singh, makes a "smart" thermometer that it sells to Americans, a kind of smartphone that then sends the measured temperatures back to Kinsa Health. Maddow showed a map of the U.S. with temperatures throughout the country. According to the *Times* article, Kinsa Health is more accurate than the Center for Disease Control and Prevention. The CDC gets its data from hospitals and clinics.

Kinsa Health provides bubble gum to entice children to take their own temperature. According to Mr. Singh, when Kinsa Health notices fever among their young customers, their personnel get in touch with their parents in case they had not noticed the change in their kids. At the time of the article and the Maddow report, Kinsa Health was collecting 25,000 readings each day. Maddow then showed us a map of Kinsa readings and coronavirus readings on a map of the US. She turned to the author of the article, Donald McNeil, seen at home via skype, and asked him if she had accurately reported his article. McNeil smiled broadly and emphatically spoke in the affirmative.

She stressed that fevers showed up before the coronavirus was tested, of course, and she got excited, saying how effective it would have been had the CDC or some other federal office used the temperatures from the smart thermometers to select people to test for coronavirus from the beginning. If positive, they could have isolated the feverish persons to prevent them from sowing the virus among others with whom they came into contact. Maddow then introduced data from Italy, talking about a small town in which they tested early and then quarantined the whole town with sterling effectiveness.

I could not follow this conversation between Maddow and McNeil, so I went on Microsoft Edge where I found an article written by Valentino Saini, "Vo', the Italian town that defeated coronavirus," dated March 24, 2020. The name of the town or "settlement," with two letters and an apostrophe is foreign to me and I assume most Americans. It is a small community of 3,000 people not far from Venice. It was the first town in Italy to report a fatality from coronavirus on February 21 and the town was quarantined two days later. A cordon was established around the town preventing anyone from entering or leaving Vo'.

By February 29, 97% of the population had been tested and after swabbing 800 per day, 3% were found to be infected, some without symptoms. People with serious cases were taken to a hospital, of course, and others were called daily at home to make sure they were abiding by instructions. Everyone was encouraged to stay at home during the period of quarantine and Saini claimed that "the strategy worked," although not that everyone was happy with it.

Here is a quote from the article: "According to Italian virologists, the 'Vo' model' shows that combining a strict quarantine with swabs, so as to identify healthy carriers, is the winning way to stop the spread of the virus—at least in smaller urban settings."

Replication?

Readers may not have needed the heading with a question mark to make them wonder what this discussion of smart thermometers and coronavirus tests has to do with a general method of reaching the truth. They do not constitute a true or Exact replication. I readily grant that point but still feel that in times of great need we have to rely on conditions not subject to the controls possible in a lab experiment. Just think how it could have benefited the U.S. if the CDC or other agencies had jumped on the pattern of fevers in the country provided by the smart thermometers and tested the fevered human for coronavirus, then isolating those with the disease.

Earlier in this book I introduced the bifurcation of Exact and Conceptual. Let us consider that using the smart thermometers and covid-19 tests as the latter of the two, a Conceptual replication, which could have provided us with a useful medical defense during this Tragic World War III against Covid-19.

The "Fraudulent Election" of 2020

I was born in Erie, Kansas on October 8, 1933 at home. The environment was rather formidable:

A. The country, including Kansas, was in the Great Depression, my parents had two daughters five and ten years older.
B. In addition, Kansas was suffering with what was called the Dust Bowl, a Drought made worse by high winds blowing dust in from Eastern Colorado and Western Kansas. I would suffer from several respiratory ailments in boyhood, including whooping cough and asthma.
C. Just as I made my entry into the world under the care of a young doctor delivering his first baby, the bed broke. This added to the normal Birth Trauma.
D. Three years later we lived in Emporia, Kansas and my father's employer, the College of Emporia, could no longer pay his salary. My mother took me to the train station to see the whistle stop of the President of the United States of America, Franklin Delano Roosevelt. He promised to help us with his New Deal. I owe it to my readers to reveal that I have been a member of Roosevelt's Democratic Party ever since.

   I make these revelations because I will make some comments that are not politically neutral, i.e., a couple of replication studies. After the 2020 elections in which Joe Biden defeated President Trump by 8,000 votes, that latter claimed the election was a fraud, that he got more votes than Biden. A tape recording was made public in which President Trump asked the Secretary of State in Georgia to find him enough votes to win.

   This was after Trump's lawyer, Rudy Giuliani, had lost battles about vote counts in courts around the country, some with judges appointed by Trump. This seemed to be a case for replication and open communication. I took my lunch break later than usual on January 4, 2021, turning to CNN at 1:00 p.m. Denver time for their continuous "Breaking News." The man on camera was from Georgia but was not the Secretary of State. He was introduced as Gabriel Sterling, Implementation Manager for Georgia's Voting System. He was holding a press conference that Monday to refute allegations made by President Donald Trump about voting in Georgia: "This is all provably false, yet the president persists," Sterling said.

   Then I heard him tell us how they had hand counted votes in the presidential election three different times and never got any significant differences. To have an Exact replication, they would have needed to have a revote and recount. But what they did with three counts makes at least two Conceptual replications. I think people who care about the truth know that these replications yielded exactly that: the truth that Biden won the State of Georgia.

What could be more important at that moment of history, just two weeks or so before the Inauguration of President Joe Biden? And yet President Trump paid no attention, two days later he encouraged non-believers to commit an Insurrection against the government, against the Capitol of the United States of America. The truth was trampled.

Chapter Sixteen
On Finding the Origins of Open Communication and Replication

The Promised Climax

I had not arrived at the promised climax when I began writing this book. No, it was not until December 1, 2020 while beginning this chapter when Mike Lampert, my Research Associate, sent me a gift that I shall always treasure and appreciate. It was the title page of a new book including the name of its author:

HOW TO MAKE
THE WORLD ADD UP

By
Tim Harford

The book was published in London by the Bridge Street Press in 2020, making it hard to get during the Pandemic, but Mike also sent copies via e-mail of pages 181 to 189. I went to work immediately on those nine pages. Page 181 began this way: "In the mid-seventeenth century, a distinction began to emerge between alchemy and a what we'd regard as modern science. It is a distinction we need to remember if we are to flourish in a world of big algorithms." Mike knew I was making a case for *replication* and *open communication* as ways to discover the truth; why then would he send me nine pages about algorithms and alchemy, the latter being the attempt to turn base metals into gold back in the 1600s, all of this written by an economic columnist for the *Financial Times* of London? Wisely, I decided to read on to learn the answer.

Harford went on to say there were many alchemists in the seventeenth century, and although some of them were men we know now as scientists, such as Isaac Newton and Robert Boyle, alchemy did not transform itself or mature into science. No, it could not achieve that status because it was conducted in *secrecy*. Sure, if you were able to make gold, what do you gain and lose by sharing the secret? A science, says Harford, requires "open debate," yes that expression appears on page 183. Is that not more or less synonymous with one of the two main expressions of this book? I got excited. Does he know the other term in my dyad? On the following page I found the answer in this key word in quotation marks: The other requirement of the new approach was "reproducibility." Harford was saying that alchemy was replaced by "open debate" and "reproducibility." We had independently come to the same basic concepts as providing the Truth.

Harford is a columnist on economic statistics for the *Financial Times* of London, not a historical scholar of science in the seventeenth century. I had been struck by a block quotation on page 185 that seemed to cement my discoveries. I checked the source and learned it had been quoted from *The Invention of Science: A New History of the Scientific Revolution*, written by David Wooton and published in London in the year 2015 by Penguin Random House UK. My daughter Emily got a copy delivered to me at home. And what a hefty tome it is: 769 pages.

I checked the Index for one of my two key terms and on p. 761 I found this entry: "replication 349, 352 353." In one of these pages Wooton refutes "sociologists of science" for saying that independent replication must be done by those associated with the original experiment. Not so, says the historian on p. 352, and I agree.

In addition, I found that Harford's block quotation from *The Invention of Science* is accurate, but a bit brief. I supply a somewhat longer version of it from p. 357:

> What killed alchemy was the insistence that experiments must be openly reported in publications which presented a clear account of what had happened, and they must then be *replicated,* preferably before independent witnesses [emphasis added]. The alchemists had pursued a secret learning, convinced that only a few were fit to have knowledge of divine secrets and that the social order would collapse if gold ceased to be in short supply. Some parts of that learning could be taken over by the advocates of the new chemistry, but much of it had to be abandoned as incomprehensible and unreproducible. Esoteric knowledge was replaced by a new form of knowledge which depended both on publication and on public or semi-public performance. A closed society was replaced by an open one.

There is a version of my words "open communication" in the expression "openly reported," and in the penultimate word itself. And there is that word "replicated" in the first sentence of the quote. Wooton had reached his position in 2015 and I came upon the same one in 2020. Did we achieve a kind of independent replication? If not, I at least gave him a kind of independent confirmation.

Upon reflection, Wooton and I were even closer in time to discovery than my being five years later. Recall that my book, *Managing Risk and Complexity through Open*

Communication and Teamwork, was published by the Purdue University Press in 2015, the same year that *The Invention of Science* was published.

That phrase Open Communication has implications for the discipline in which I found myself helping establish. I was recruited into the field of Speech, even though my main concentration at the doctoral level used the label Organizational Communication. By my work at NASA, I came to find reasons to recommend Open Communication. And in combining those words with Replication in this book, this pursuit of wisdom, I came to replicate or confirm the findings of the Historian of Science who had found the same set of concepts established Science. Ironically, I discovered replication from the Chemistry Department at Purdue and Wooton discovered the use of replication and open communication helped found the Science of Chemistry.

To all those colleagues in the field of Communication, rejoice in the revolution that produced your new discipline, and come to accept the high responsibility of the importance of Open Communication to Science, Truth, and the good of society.

Seeking Wisdom and Wisdom Itself

In this my final chapter I want to borrow again a quotation from the *Dictionary of Philosophy*, one used in the Foreword: Philosophy is "both the seeking of wisdom and the wisdom itself." This book does both, that is, while trying to find wise applications of replication and open communication, forces I discovered on my own, I happened on the discovery that my two terms are themselves wisdom, the conditions necessary to give birth to science.

This provides me answers to give my friend the philosopher, Gregory Desilet, who said I could not consider anything other than an Exact replication. That is what produces Exact science; replications with fewer degrees than perfection can still produce high probabilities and accurate predictions. Replicating Capote's methods gave me a different set of facts; my facts were confirmed by replication by an independent fact-checker, a research editor at a magazine. Second opinions are not perfect replications, sometimes they use additional tests to be more exacting, but they do seem to benefit patients most of the time. Allowing for Conceptual replications encourages citizens to use the concept in say, getting two bids, asking more than one merchant for a price and other relevant issues important to a transaction.

Recall the first and most Exact case of replication: the replication of lab experiments that failed, leading the Chemistry Department to rescind a doctoral degree. Before making the decision and asking the university-wide faculty, including me, to vote for rescinding the degree, they gathered additional, circumstantial evidence. Recall that they found the student had a missing year on his Curriculum Vitae at an Ivy League

University; he declined to come back to Purdue to discuss the replication failure,, but bought copies of his transcript. They also informed us that he had forged the lab analyst's forms. The chemists know they must make rhetorical appeals even in a laboratory decision. Rhetoric is part of science, and other uses of replication.

Part of me wanted to quit there, but the reader will recall that the elective basis of my doctorate a Purdue University was in a new field called Organizational Communication. I have written three books about the subject, two about NASA and one about the Kent State University tragedy, plus co-editing an "org com" book about theory and practice. While reading the rest of the nine pages by Harford I came upon an interesting argument by analogy on page 185: "The likes of Google and Target are no more keen to share their datasets and algorithms than Newton was to share his alchemical experiments." Harford goes on to mention Facebook and other organizations that are in the alchemy business, i.e., secrecy. Interestingly, about ten days after I read these words, Facebook was charged by the Federal Trade Commission with alleged violations of the Antitrust Laws. Harford's book thus gives more than one boost to the importance of communication: both *open* and *closed*.

I must conclude that the Wooton book and the Tompkins book *independently replicated each other*. Harford seems to have accepted and repeated Wooton's claims, while my book replicated Wooton without being aware of his earlier conclusions reached by means of historical research. That they were done independently from different academic perspectives makes them even more convincing.

Finally, I do not wish to sound provincial after these universal discoveries, but it must be observed that students of higher education have an academic revolution to study. Those women and men who participated in the change from the Discipline of Speech to that of Communication can share in a sense of accomplishment. Those who have joined the field since then should also feel a sense of academic pride. The book in your hand at this moment urges you to understand the importance of Open Communication, and how it must be taught as one of the two vital factors providing the truth, the aim of all academic efforts.

Addendum

The rest of the book was completed yesterday, March 23, 2021. For the past few weeks, my wife Elaine read the first draft aloud so that she could help me find typos and better ways of expressing the truth. Her contribution was essential. In the second week of January, I had two appointments at the Franklin Center of our local Kaiser Permanente facilities. One was with my eye doctor and the other was to have a CT scan of my liver. The eye doctor told me what I already knew: My Macular Degeneration continues to advance. I can no longer drive a car, not even a few blocks on a sunny morning. I have increased the font size on e-mail and the text of this book. The nurse in my surgeon's office called to say that the new cancer on the left lobe of my liver discovered six months ago at one centimeter in size has grown to five centimeters.

Rene quoted Dr. Stangl as saying that is "quick," and thus may make it difficult to treat with chemotherapy. He would understand if I wished to avoid the pain and hospitalization of my last treatment. At the same time, he hoped that I will submit to another chemotherapy treatment. Part of me wanted to say "No," to begin enjoying the martinis and red wine I gave up six years ago when Dr. Stangl found the cancer and first treated it. But the other voice won. I showed up for the treatment that was scheduled two weeks later. In the double race against time, I hoped to finish the writing of this book with Elaine's help and send it off to the publisher via the good work of my friend Gary Moore.

I must break in here with the latest medical news: In mid-April of 2021 I had another CT scan of my liver and the results are that the mass has been reduced from five centimeters to two. Plus, no new masses were detected. It is no longer a double race.

Research Associates and other Helpers

I originally wrote a chapter for this book about my retirement from teaching at the University of Colorado at Boulder in 1998. I loved teaching but the academic politics at CU were worse than I had experienced anywhere else. There is an old saying that academic politics are so nasty because so little is at stake. My wife Elaine and I moved to a loft in downtown Denver we loved immediately after retiring.

We went to church one Sunday morning in 1998 at the beautiful St. John's Episcopal Cathedral. A guest speaker during a break was a tall handsome man named Tom Luehrs, the Director of the St. Francis Center, a large day shelter for homeless people in Denver, only eight blocks from our loft in Brooks Tower. Tom was calling for volunteers to work in the shelter.

St. Francis Center

I showed up the next day and was trained to be a volunteer. I was taught by Carla Slatt-Burns that *homeless* is an adjective, not a noun. I have not used it as a noun in the 22 years since then. Volunteering was a second calling. I loved helping our homeless "guests" as we call them. I also did research and wrote a book that was published in 2009, *Who is My Neighbor?* Yes, that question is part of the Parable of the Good Samaritan.

While still at St. John's I indulged religion for the first time, taking a four-year course called Education for Ministry, or EFM. The premise was that we are not all fit to become Ministers, but we can and ought to adopt a ministry. I discovered the monumental research of a British religious scholar named Karen Armstrong. She was chosen for a TED Talk and used the money to finance a gathering of leaders from all the world's religions. The task she gave them was to find concurrence on the most important value or teaching they shared. It turned out to be *compassion*. Armstrong coined the phrase "Discipline of Compassion." It moved and inspired me so much I came up with a slightly different phrase for the St. Francis Center that I am still proud of, that is, the "Collective Discipline of Compassion."

Trinity United Methodist Church

The Dean of the Cathedral moved on, and a new Dean drove us away. In 2000 my wife Elaine was offered a job at the most beautiful church in Denver, Trinity United Methodist Church, built in 1888 with handsome stone in a Gothic Revival style. Located on Broadway at 18th, it is within walking distance for us on a nice day. We have been members since attending our first Sunday service twenty years ago, reveling in the internal beauty of the church. The minister, Dr. Darrell Mount, hypnotized us, and we enjoyed being members of the Trinity Academy, a senior Sunday School.

Trinity Academy

Elaine and I became dues-paying members of the Trinity Academy, the adult Sunday School meeting from 9:30 to 10:30 between the eight and eleven o'clock services. The eighty members were led by a team without formal titles: Nita DiPiero, care and concern; David Jackson, finance; Mary Jackson, membership and social events; Paula Kaufman, opening and closing sessions; Jan Shellhammer, communications; Jan Silverstein, program subcommittee lead. Amy Lorton and Miriam Slejko were added to the team for 2021.

The team brought in professors of some sort of theology or religious studies from universities in and around Denver. Members might hear a close reading of a text in the New Testament, the history of Judaism, or Comparative Religion. Elaine and I became dedicated members, talking to the speakers at times before going up to the beautiful sanctuary for the 11:00 service conducted by the Senior Minister, Dr. Darrell Mount, whose doctorate was in engineering. Michael Dent took over after Mount retired, and now that role is played by Ken Brown, a striking African American leader and preacher. After the 11:00 service Elaine and I would invariably walk across the street into the famous Brown Palace Hotel, often with Lorraine Gregg, into the Ship Tavern for lunch.

I became the link or liaison between the St. Francis Center and the Trinity United Methodist Church. I began volunteering at SFC in October of 1998 and joined TUMC not long after that. In February of 2005, I was asked by a minister to organize and moderate a series of four programs about homelessness at Trinity: The Faces of Homelessness. The forums were held on Thursday evenings at Trinity in February.

The first forum began at 7:00 p.m., on Thursday January 20, 2005, in Fellowship Hall of Trinity United Methodist Church. Reverend Carlisle introduced me as the Moderator and Organizer. The first speaker was Tom Luehrs, Executive Director of the St. Francis Center for thirteen years and the Head of the Metro Denver Homeless Initiative. Bernie O'Connell, an outreach worker at SFC was the second speaker. Third was Tom Jensen, a music director of the Junior Symphony Guild Orchestra who discover a homeless boy who played for us at the Trinity Forum. We then found housing for the boy and his mother. As the fourth speaker, I explained we experienced "compassion fatigue" while getting the homeless family housed.

The other three forums had excellent speakers and were well attended, particularly for those cold February Thursdays. The listing of all speakers and summaries of their presentations can be found in my book: *Who is My Neighbor? Communicating and Organizing to End Homelessness* (2009).

Strengthening the link between TUMC and SFC were the actions of Pam Hubbard, a member of Trinity. In 2016, Pam sought me out to have lunch at the Delectable Egg. She wanted to talk to me about the possibility of serving as a volunteer at SFC. While at that lunch she explained that she was a retired social worker with a Master of Social Work degree and thought she could be of service at the shelter. I gave her a copy of *Who is My Neighbor?* As I recall, I helped her start in the fall of 2016, and she became a highly valued volunteer member at the shelter. She and her husband Bob became friends of ours.

Pam, in turn, brought Rev. Deb Meyer to the shelter on a day I happened to be there. Yes, the Director of Servant Ministries at Trinity came to the homeless shelter presumably looking for ways to become a servant to people who needed her. She found them and established an Allyship to work on helping homeless people, but the coronavirus shut down the church and made even meetings problematic.

The Allyship met regularly via e-mail under Deb's leadership. In addition to Deb, members were Jan Silverstein, a leader of the Trinity Academy, Pam Hubbard of Trinity and St. Francis Center, Phil Tompkins of Trinity and the shelter, and later Joan Maybury was added to the group. Joan is a retired nurse, member of Trinity, volunteer at SFC, and a resident, with her husband Phillip., in Brooks Tower, the building in downtown Denver where Elaine and I have lived since 1998.

Deb amazed me by her leadership. She did a job of research before teaching the members what we needed to know to improve life for homeless people. Denver is a state capital and a big city; she found out what agencies in government could be of help to the Allyship's mission. She would give directions to the members about phone calls to offices and people that could do good. I will give an example below.

I got the word from Director Luehrs on March 18, 2020 that all volunteers seventy and older should not come to work at the St. Francis Center until the Pandemic ended.

For almost 22 years, volunteering there had been one of the most gratifying experiences. I enjoyed this second calling, after playing the role of professor for most of my life. I have been called back since then after 51 weeks as I write on March 19, 2021. During the layoff I did continue to make trips to the shelter, wearing my mask of course, with donations and other goods from Brooks Tower where we live.

While driving to SFC with donations during the lock down, or shut down, during 2020 I began to see tents popping up on sidewalks in the neighborhood of the shelter. I talked to Tom Luehrs who has been around for a long time and had never seen anything like it. There were "encampments" in other parts of Denver, e.g., near the State Capitol building. Tom told me that there was an SOS movement to do something about them. The acronym stood for Safe Outdoor Spaces. They would provide toilets, drinking water, and other survival services as well as clean ups.

I sent an e-mail message to the Allyship regulars, Deb, Jan Silverstein, Pam, and Joan about SOS. Deb went to work on it, found out which city departments would have to administer it and which ones would have to enact it. Soon we had a couple of SOS spots in the city. Not enough, of course, but Deb had done a great job mobilizing support for them.

Another example of how I got to play the liaison between the church and the shelter was a phone call I got from the Chair of Trinity's Second Century Foundation, Gary Moore. He called me up in 2018, as I recall, and asked me for a tour of the St. Francis Center. He explained that the Second Century Foundation is the chief financial charity of TUMC, and he had heard about my work and wanted to learn more. I happily accepted, giving him my quasi-academic lecture as we went into the Storage Room at the front of the building where guests store their few belongings in a large, standard garbage bag with nametag. I showed him the alphabetical files of U.S. Mail addressed to our guests. Then on to the Men's Showers—but not the Women's—and the Clothing Room where guests could get a complete set of clothing, inner and outer ware, after earning a Clothing Slip by doing a chore for us such as sweeping, mopping, cleaning toilets or sinks. On to the laundry and donation room. He then took me to his club, the Denver Athletic Club, for a sumptuous lunch.

In fact, I remember being treated to a couple of lunches there. He got me to talk about my academic career, and he told me about his business career in which he rose to the top of a business firm and then became its owner. Trinity's Second Century Fund, drawing upon Gary's business knowledge and experience, wound up providing financial help for the shelter. Gary and I became friends and then he made an unusual request.

"I want you to send me a short letter including a story after every Friday that you work at the shelter."

"Why?" I asked.

"Because you had all kinds of stories you told me while giving me the tour of the shelter. We could put out a book that I would publish, and we could give copies to the shelter as well as whatever income it brings in."

Stories from the Shelter

I quickly learned I enjoyed every step of looking and listening for stories, taking notes on my work-slip as I had while writing *Who is My Neighbor?* This time, however, I sent each story via e-mail to Gary. He gave them titles and did some minor editing. He used a story by Pam Hubbard, the Trinity member and SFC volunteer, and a poem by Frank Russell Lewis, a fellow volunteer at the SFC and a good friend of mine who was once homeless himself. There is another poem in the book, "The Sojourner," written by Gary's wife, Jane Costain.

There is also a narrative written by me that summarizes a presentation made to the Trinity Academy on January 5, 2020 by Deb Meyer, a member of the ministry at Trinity United Methodist Church. She selected her own ministerial title, one I appreciate more than any such expression I have ever heard: "Director of Servant Ministries." I still love it! After my summary of her talk to the Academy she wrote this:

> I think you captured the essence of my perspective that the
> equilibrium between theology and praxis is righting, that the
> Christ-like is more than studying God . . .to be like Christ requires
> that we put our understandings into action, going in faith to the
> people and places where we're not so comfortable.
> Blessings,
>
> Deb Meyer

As pointed out above, Deb helped us put faith into action assisting the homeless people of Denver.

Gary got the Outskirts Press to publish the book at his expense. It came out in early 2020, just before the coronavirus shut down Trinity church and Academy. He gave 30 copies to the St. Francis Center for them to give to potential donors or others. He gave me some and I sold a few in the Trinity Academy before we were shut down. All proceeds of *Stories of the Shelter* went to the St. Francis Center.

Post-Retirement Colleagues and Research Associates

When I retired, Elaine kept teaching at CU Boulder for a couple of years after we moved to the loft in downtown Denver. I stopped going to academic conventions and felt isolated from that part of the world despite writing books and giving lectures. Dr. Omar Swartz invited me to walk a couple of blocks across Cherry Creek to the CU Denver campus where he has an office as Associate Professor of Humanities and Social Sciences. He has a law degree from Duke University (magna cum laude) and a Ph.D. in Communication from Purdue University.

He invited me to give lectures to classes, state conventions, and other gatherings. But he also became an informal research associate, helping me find academic articles that he sent to me electronically via e-mail. He would let me know when I could find a scholarly book I wanted in the CU Denver Library by walking across the Creek. If not, he would get it on interlibrary loan. Our families experienced social events together. How many times did he help with research for this book? I know it was plenty. He read the first draft and spent hours with me on ZOOM making helpful suggestions for improvement.

Michael Lampert entered the narrative of this book as an undergraduate student in a couple of my classes at SUNY Albany during the 1970s. He kept in touch after moving on to the Harvard University Law School. He wound up at a law firm doing commercial litigation and arbitration with offices in New York and London. Since retiring he acts as an independent arbitrator, a mediator, and teaches as an adjunct at a law school. He continues to write two articles a year and speaks at continuing legal education programs at Harvard.

He is something of a genius finding things an author needs electronically, he in New York City and sending them to me in Denver. I have mentioned that work several times in the text of this book, but not nearly often enough. The climax of his help provided the climax of this book. He discovered the references in my final chapter that show by historical work that Open Communication and Replication first came together in the 1600s, creating the Truth known as Science. I cannot thank him enough for this discovery—and to understand my search for truth well enough to know when he had found it.

This coming Friday, March 26, 2021, because of my limited vision, a long-time friend and colleague as volunteer at the St. Francis Center, Patricia Tomcho, will pick me up at 8:30 and bring me back home at 2:00 from the St. Francis Center. I want to thank her and hope we have many more of those rides and days at the shelter.

Index

D

E

F

M

N

O

T

U

V

W

Z

CPSIA information can be obtained
at www.ICGtesting.com
Printed in the USA
BVHW022113060721
611232BV00014B/1517